MISCARRIAGE OF A DREAM

WHAT TO DO WHEN GOD'S PLANS DON'T MATCH YOURS

KRISTI LARRABEE

Published by Author Academy Elite
P.O. Box 43, Powell, OH 43035

Paperback: 978-1-64746-501-8
Hardback: 978-1-64746-502-5
E-book: 978-1-64746-503-2
(LCCN): 2020917632

Dedication:

To my wonderful husband, Jason, who has been my rock throughout this crazy journey, and to our miracle, Caden, who made the journey worth every painful step.

TABLE OF CONTENTS

INTRODUCTION

Dreams. We all have them. Plans. We all make them. Some we've had for years, others for only a short time. Some are for ourselves, and others are for our loved ones. Sometimes those plans come relatively easily into fruition, and sometimes they don't. Sometimes they die—literally or figuratively. What are we supposed to do when they die? How do we handle the jumble of emotions that sometimes threaten to overtake us? How are we supposed to know whether to keep pushing toward that dream or just give up and get a different one? I will help you answer these questions. You see, I have been on a journey through the wasteland of miscarried dreams myself. A journey I never thought I would have to navigate. When my dream died, I found myself navigating treacherous terrain littered with the obstacles of crushing disappointment, shattering grief, hope deferred, and the miry muck of the pit of despair. These are obstacles we all face when our dreams die. But there is also hope. Hope that one day, no matter how great the odds, our dreams will come to pass.

I spent years trudging along this path, wondering, "Why is this happening?" "Where are you, God?" "When will this end?" "When will my dream finally happen?" "*Will* it ever happen?" And then, finally, the lesson of acceptance sprouted from the seed planted in the soil of my heart. Soil that had been broken, tilled, and raked into the ability to die to my own wants and agenda, and bear the fruit of the One to whom I should have yielded my plans from the beginning. I wish I could have learned that lesson through less painful circumstances, but oftentimes our best lessons come through situations we were not expecting to go through.

My journey was a seven-year period of infertility and recurrent pregnancy loss. However, the word "miscarriage" does not only apply to the loss of a baby. It is also defined as, "the failure to attain the just, right, or desired result."[1] So, any dream that hasn't panned out the way you hoped, or seems to have died, could be considered a miscarried dream.

For you, it may be a dream you've had since childhood that just won't happen no matter what you do. A child that has strayed away from the path you hoped they would follow and has instead gotten caught in the trap of addiction. A major health diagnosis that sends your life into a tailspin. A career path that was progressing as planned, now suddenly derailed. A premature death of a friend, spouse, parent, or child that causes you to question everything you ever believed. A marriage that started out so loving and delightful that has degenerated into ruins. So many different possible journeys, but the final destination is the same: Acceptance of and full trust in God's will and plan for your life or the lives of the ones you love.

I am still making my way through this journey. Acceptance is not a one-time destination, but a daily attitude of putting God's plan before our own. I have, however, gained some wisdom through the hills and valleys I have travelled thus far. Wisdom that I hope, when shared, will help others navigate their own journey through the wasteland of miscarried dreams.

There are many ways in which a dream can die. It could be that the dream or idea isn't part of God's plan for your life or your loved one's life, period. It could also be that the time is not right for the dream to happen now. Growth and maturity must first be cultivated by the Holy Spirit in order for you to be ready for everything the dream entails. Lastly, it could be that the dream you have, and the plan God has for you are similar, but the path to getting there and the results don't end up looking the way you expected.

All of these scenarios can lead to a whole host of emotions that take us on a rollercoaster ride as we try to work our way through them. Disillusionment, fear, anger, discouragement, sadness, hope, and determination to name only a few. There are also many ways that our walk with God can get derailed during times like these. We can choose to blame God, to push Him away during our hard times instead of turning toward Him, or even decide to disconnect ourselves from Him altogether and abandon our faith. We can become angry, bitter, and resentful when our dreams seemingly die.

Proverbs 13:12a says, "Hope deferred makes the heart sick..." This is so very true. We can get mired down in this boggy ground and the angst it produces if we aren't careful. "Angst" is defined as "a feeling of deep anxiety, dread, or anguish."[2] It is "a feeling of persistent worry or tension, of apprehension or insecurity."[3] These feelings arise from the internal pressure that mounts when things don't go the way we want them to. We feel like a failure. We worry that we won't measure up to our idea of success in our lives. We worry people will judge us as failures if we or our children aren't living up to the picture of happiness, we've dreamed up for them.

How will I help you navigate this treacherous ground? How will I help you move from angst to acceptance in your life? First, the angst that results from trying to live our plans and dreams in our own strength and timing must be addressed. Then, when we are aware of the problem, we will learn the process of correcting it. Finally, we will see what our lives can look like when we finally come to an acceptance of God's plans and are able to live the abundant lives He has for us. Proverbs 16:9 says, "In his heart a man plans his course, but the Lord determines his steps." There is peace in this if we can work our way around to yielding our plans and dreams to the Lord.

PART I

ANGST

1

BEST LAID PLANS

My name is Kristi and I am a control-oholic. It has been approximately five minutes since my last attempt to take control of my life. I am a planner. I like to have a mental road map for how things are going to go in my life so I can be prepared. That goes for general life plans and also my agenda within each day. I will be the first to admit that when those plans are disrupted, changed, or otherwise compromised, I really don't like it. At all.

I can recall a specific example of this from several years ago. I was driving home from work just before the dinner hour, mentally mapping out what I needed to get done when I got home. Get my stuff unloaded and put away, feed the dogs, throw something together for dinner, pick up the clutter in the kitchen before my husband got home from work, etc.

Well, imagine my surprise when my husband was already home when I got there! It was much earlier than he normally comes home. This small thing totally threw off my plan, and I actually felt myself getting upset and annoyed. Irrationally, of course, because he hadn't done anything wrong by coming home early and helping out with things. It was simply that him being there threw off my plans, and that created a feeling of angst inside me. I got a little snappy towards him at first. Then I realized what I was doing and had to apologize and explain that I needed a minute to readjust my plan for the evening.

It seems silly to be so affected by such a small thing, but some people, myself included, feel a sense of anxiety when their plans, or mental roadmaps, don't proceed as planned. It can cause meltdowns in children who don't yet have the verbal and emotional skills to cope with these feelings. If I'm honest, there have been times this has happened to me, and I had a meltdown. Not outwardly toward others, but toward, my Heavenly Father.

In his book, *What Your Explosive Child is Trying to Tell You*, Douglas A. Riley says some people, "Have an unusually strong need to know what is going to happen, because not knowing creates anxiety. This drives them to make predictions, which in turn fills up their roadmap and makes them feel safe."[1] I would venture to say that a lot of us are like this to one degree or another. We like to feel a sense of control over how things happen. Some of our roadmaps or plans are flexible, with a few major points filled in along the way with plenty of room for improvisation if things change course. Others are tighter, filling in more details with less wiggle room. Some people are much more easily able to roll with the punches if things don't go as planned, others are filled with tension and anxiety at the first sign of something unexpected happening.

I had a general plan for my life mapped out at a fairly early age. I would graduate high school, go to college, get married, spend a few years working at a then-undetermined career, and then have children—two for sure, maybe three. That was it. Fulfill this simple plan and live happily ever after. I'd have all my kids by the time I was thirty and spend the rest of my life being a mom. Maybe I would still work part-time, but my career was never going to be the focus of my life. Family was.

It was all I ever wanted. And for a while, my plan seemed to be going pretty well. I may have had a little trouble figuring out exactly what I wanted to study in college, but I landed on dental hygiene (after a couple failed attempts at other majors), and that ended up fitting me well. I married Jason at age twenty-one, checking the next milestone off my mental list.

After we'd been married two years, we decided it was time to start trying for the family we both wanted. When we got pregnant on the first try, we were both pleasantly surprised. We hadn't expected it to happen that quickly. We were thrilled, of course, and told everyone we knew. The last thing on either of our minds was the possibility of that baby not being born perfectly healthy eight months later.

Unfortunately, that was not to be. As the years passed and I suffered miscarriage after miscarriage, I felt more and more out of control of my life—more and more like a failure. This was not how things were supposed to happen! I had a plan, darn it! Why was it that the one thing I most wanted in the whole world was the one thing I couldn't seem to have? It certainly seemed simple enough for everyone else I knew. Surely there must be something I was doing wrong. There must be something I could fix in to finally make my dreams of a family a reality. Right? Wrong.

I am not only a planner, but I'm also fixer too. God help me! If I or someone I know or love has a problem, my first instinct is to try to fix it. I suppose it goes back to the whole control-oholic thing. Doing something to help in a problem situation makes me feel in control of the problem. Whether that something helps or not, at least I am *doing* something.

Really though, there is only one true fixer of things, and His name is Jesus. It's just that His fixes don't always look like what we think they should look like. In fact, they almost never look like what we think or expect them to. I guess that's supposed to be part of the adventure of living life with Jesus. Except, I never was very big on adventure! I prefer knowing what to expect.

It took several years for me to finally accept that none of this was really in my control. What happened in my womb was going to happen, no matter what I ate or did, or didn't do to overexert myself. I couldn't make a baby stay alive. There was nothing I could do about any of it. And I was probably never going to find out the one thing I wanted to know above all else: Why was this happening to me? Modern medicine could not find anything wrong with me or my husband. There were no answers as to why we lost our babies to help me have closure. It had just happened.

* * *

Making plans gives us a sense of control over our lives. One of the things that can lead to some serious and unnecessary angst, however, is getting ahead of God's plans for our lives. We can get ourselves into situations we should never have been in at all, or get ahead of God's perfect timing, making things a lot more difficult for ourselves. We can set ourselves up for failure when we do this. James 4: 13-15 says, "Now listen, you who say, 'Today or tomorrow we will go to this or that city, spend a year there, carry on business and make money.' Why, you do not even know what will happen tomorrow. You are a mist that appears for a little while and then vanishes. Instead you ought to say, 'If it is the Lord's will, we will live and do this or that.'"

Abraham and Sarah are a prime example of what can happen when we get ahead of God's plan and try to take control ourselves. Their story is in Genesis 15-21. When Abraham was around the age of 75 and Sarah 65, the Lord told him that he would have a son to be his heir and become the father of many nations, with descendants greater than the stars in the sky. Sounds great, right? Well, apparently, He didn't mean this was going to happen right away.

After about ten years, Sarah was getting impatient. I mean, can you blame her? She was 75 years old, after all. She said to Abraham, "The Lord has kept me from having children. Go, sleep with my maidservant; perhaps I can build a family through her." So, instead of waiting for God's promise to be fulfilled in His own perfect timing, Sarah took matters into her own hands and enacted the Mesopotamian custom of a barren wife providing children for her husband through her maidservant, Hagar.

What could possibly go wrong with this ingenious plan? Well, Hagar began to despise Sarah as soon as she got pregnant. This caused conflict and hostility between them, which Sarah blamed on Abraham! This animosity went on for years. After Sarah finally gave birth to Isaac, when Hagar's son, Ishmael, was a teenager, Sarah sent them both away, feeling Ishmael a threat to Isaac's inheritance.

The angel of the Lord had spoken to Hagar when she was first pregnant, telling her that He would make Ishmael into a great nation because he was Abraham's son. He also told her Ishmael would live in hostility toward all his brothers. They settled in the desert and Ishmael grew up to be the father of the modern Arab nations, who are still in conflict with each other and the descendants of Isaac, the Israeli nation to this day. Hostility passed from generation to generation, all because Sarah couldn't wait for the Lord's timing and plan.

All the conflict between these nations, throughout history until now, was caused by this one mistake. One woman getting ahead of God's plan. Talk about a sobering thought. *Our impatience, fear, pride, rebellion, and need to control* could get us into big trouble and have ramifications we could never anticipate. Ramifications that can span generations. God tells us to wait on Him for a reason.

If you find yourself struggling with the need to control things, you are certainly not alone. It is human nature to want to be in control of our own lives. People have been making that choice and suffering the consequences for it ever since Adam and Eve. However, that was not the way God intended it to be when He created them. His intention was for humanity to live in freedom by submitting ourselves to His control, not so that He could exercise some unhealthy dominance over us, but because He is all-knowing and all-loving. In His sovereignty, He is able to take into account so much more information than we could ever know about how different situations we encounter would be good or bad for us.

We think we have all the answers and can make informed decisions. However, we cannot know how those decisions will cause a domino effect in our lives and the lives of others for good or ill. Only God can know that. It is essential to come to the place of surrendering our need to control things to Him. This takes trust, which is difficult to cultivate in a world where we see things going so apparently wrong, to our way of thinking. It's easy to get disillusioned and wonder where God even is in the happenings of the world around us, and in our own lives when we don't see our dreams coming true.

If you find you may need additional help dealing with your inborn need for control, I recommend an old book, written back in the early nineties by Christian psychotherapist, Dr. Les Carter, as a starting place. It's out of print now but can be purchased used on Amazon. It is called, *Imperative People*[2], and will be a valuable resource alongside this book if you wish to begin your journey toward learning to identify areas where you may be trying to exert too much control in your life. I won't be delving into that aspect of things in this book as much as learning to let go and trust God's plan for your future.

So, am I saying it's bad to make plans? No. It is not necessarily wrong to want to have a plan or dream for your life or the lives of your loved ones. What *is* wrong is *relying on that plan for your sense of control and safety*. What is wrong is not taking God's plan into account, and the fact that it may look different than yours. The chasm between our hopes and expectations and what reality ends up being, is a place that is easily filled with tension and anxiety, which can lead to anger and bitterness if we're not careful. It is this chasm, however, that can be the area God will use for our greatest growth.

Go ahead and be a planner but seek God for your plans. It says in Proverbs 16:9 that "The mind of man plans his way, but the Lord directs his steps." It's important to learn to be flexible, so when unexpected twists come along your path, and they will come, you can roll with the punches. It is challenging to loosen the tight grip we want to have on our control over our lives, much less let go of it entirely. Trying to release the lives of our children or spouse, our business or vocation, or simply the manner in which we live, into the hands of God? Terrifying! *Learning to let go is a process, not a one-time action.* It is a daily, lifelong process by which we decide to lay down our right and desire to control our lives or the lives of others.

Are you ready to begin this process together? It won't be easy. It takes a lot of heart work to finally learn to surrender to the Lord and say, "Your kingdom come. Your will be done." If you will put in the effort now, it will be well worth the peace it will bring you.

DISCUSSION QUESTIONS

1. Are you a person who likes to plan or control things or do you roll with the punches?

2. Can you remember a time when an unexpected disruption of your plans or "roadmap" caused a negative reaction from you?

3. Does the thought of giving up control of things in your life bring up feelings of anxiety in you?

2

WHEN PLANS FAIL

Our dreams and plans don't always go the way we hope. Sometimes they seemingly fail. There are a few different reactions people have when they experience a setback in their plans. They may:

1. Refuse to accept the failure and keep trying to achieve the goal they are striving for.
2. See themselves as a failure, get discouraged, and give up.
3. Get angry and blame God

Some of us may fall solely into one of these camps, while others may react in any or all of these ways depending on the circumstances.

I have reacted in all three of these ways for different plans that have gone awry. I can be a very stubborn person (don't tell my husband I'm admitting that), and in most situations, I don't easily give up on something I want. There have been times I let fear discourage me more quickly and have given up after one failure, though in the end, God helped me to have the courage to try again.

In early December of 2002, I suspected I might be pregnant. We had only just started trying, so I didn't want to get my hopes up too high. I thought it would take longer than a month of trying before we succeeded. I took the test while my husband was at work, just in case I was wrong. It was the longest three minutes of my life up to that point as I waited to find out whether or not our lives were about to change forever.

Sure enough, the test was positive. Pure, unadulterated joy and wonder swept through me. I lay a hand on my belly. A belly that looked exactly the same as it had only moments before, yet somehow seemed different now that I knew there was a tiny life growing inside it. A perfect mix of Jason and me. I wondered if it would be a boy or a girl and imagined what it was going to be like to raise them. I had visions of playing catch in the yard with a little boy that looked like Jason. Of teaching a little girl to figure skate or bake cookies. Scenes of bedtime stories, skinned knees, and snuggles during midnight thunderstorms danced through my head one after another. I was so excited to have my chance to be the mother I always wanted to be!

The joy and anticipation I felt at the sight of that positive pregnancy test turned to anxiety when I started spotting a week later. It was the first time the thought entered my mind that my hopes and dreams for the child I carried might be in danger of failing. Although the nurse at my obstetrician's office reassured me several times that spotting didn't always lead to a miscarriage, I couldn't shake the sense of impending doom that settled into my heart. That feeling was confirmed when I started feeling sick with cramps on Christmas Eve at Jason's family celebration at his parents' house. After some debate, we'd decided to think positively and tell his family about the baby, but no one knew about the spotting or how preoccupied my mind was with worry over it and how sick I was feeling.

On Christmas Day, we were home alone, having celebrated with our families already. All thoughts of holiday cheer were long forgotten as the painful cramps worsened throughout the morning. Jason knew I wasn't feeling well, but wasn't worried because he thought that was normal in early pregnancy. While he spent the day woodworking in the garage, I lay in bed with what became regular, agonizing pains in my belly. There I was, twenty-three years old, my first time being pregnant, with no clue what was happening to me, out of my mind with agony and fear. I knew something was terribly wrong, but didn't know exactly what was happening or what to do about it. I was pretty sure I was having a miscarriage, but until I started bleeding in earnest, I wasn't entirely sure. Even while it was happening, I didn't want to believe it was really possible I was losing my baby. My beautiful dream was crumbling before my very eyes. I spent the day alternately crying from pain and fear, and trying to escape into the oblivion of sleep.

By the evening it was over and I knew for sure I had lost the baby. All I could think was, how could this happen? I was just deliriously happy at the thought of having a baby only days before, and now I was sitting in my bathroom, alone, shell-shocked at the loss of my dream, totally baffled that this could happen. This possibility had never even occurred to me. I was pregnant, ergo, of course I would have a healthy baby. No other possible alternative existed in my mind.

At this point, a very pervasive sensation of unreality stole over me. I had lost a baby that had not seemed quite real to me yet. I'd barely had enough time to get used to the idea of being pregnant. I was only six weeks pregnant on the day of the miscarriage, so I wasn't showing, nor had I felt the baby move. I hadn't even experienced many pregnancy symptoms yet. It was almost as if my pregnancy had been a weird dream, and then it was suddenly over.

After a while, I left the bathroom and told my husband that I'd had a miscarriage. His reply was, "Oh well, we'll just try again." He didn't even appear upset. It was like we were just discussing the weather. At the time, I was hurt by what I saw as a flippant response to losing our baby. Years later, I came to find out that Jason didn't know any more about the process of having a miscarriage than I did at that time, so he hadn't realized what I went through that day. He said that when I came out of the bathroom and told him, he felt shocked even though he didn't show it outwardly. He wanted to remain strong and positive for me, which is why he said we would just try again. It saddens me that I allowed a misunderstanding to keep us from coming together in our loss. Instead, I went back into our bedroom and cried for the loss of our dream by myself.

After the miscarriage, a new and very uncomfortable sense of vulnerability entered my heart. It was horrible to feel that absolute sense of powerlessness over the circumstances of my life. Especially for a control freak such as myself. The sense of security I had derived from making my plans was destroyed. It left the raw center of my heart feeling totally exposed. Bad things could happen and I couldn't always stop them.

Of course, logically, I knew bad things happened in life, but that was the first time it had happened to *me*. It didn't happen to someone I knew, but to *me*. I was young enough to still have a fair amount of the youthful feeling of invincibility left in me. Nothing terrible would happen to *me*. That stuff happened to other people. The feeling of safety that I had taken for granted in my life was badly shaken. Life was suddenly out of my control. Before I could fully get used to the idea that I was going to have a baby, it was gone. And there was nothing I could have done to stop it. It was completely out of my control. *I* was out of control. Floating in a weightless abyss of utter disbelief that my plans and dreams could end up like this.

So, what did I do? Did I take the time to process those feelings properly and learn from them? Did I grieve for the loss of my child and dream? No, I did not. I got up, dusted myself off, and put it immediately behind me. We would try again. Everything would work out next time. This was just a temporary setback—a one-time thing. Surely this wouldn't happen again, right? In fact, just to be really sure it wouldn't happen again, I even prayed that I wouldn't get pregnant again until the time was right for us to have a baby, rather than losing another pregnancy.

I was in a bit of denial at this point in my journey. Really, I was stuffing my feelings—a bad habit that we will discuss in greater depth later on. I was so focused on trying to get pregnant again, that I did not even allow myself to feel the grief of losing my baby. I simply soldiered on. Things hadn't turned out as planned, but I wasn't going to let that stop me from pushing *full steam ahead* toward my dream of a family. Was that right or wrong? Isn't perseverance under trials a good thing? Aren't we supposed to press on toward the goal, no matter what happens?

Yes, I believe all those things are true, with one caveat: *within the realm of God's plan.* There is no sense in pressing on toward a goal or dream if it's not in alignment with God's plan. Psalm 127:1a says, "Unless the Lord builds the house, its builders labor in vain." If we build our plans and dreams without first consulting God about them, we can get stuck laboring in vain for something He doesn't have planned for us.

This can also happen with our loved ones. We have many dreams for them and how we think their lives should go, what our definition of success looks like for them. We can labor in vain trying to make their lives what we think they should be, but what about God's plans? What if it takes a long season of what appears to be really bad things happening in their lives to bring them to the place that God wants them to be in order for them to become the kind of people He wants them to be?

When Jason and I decided to start a family, we did not even think to consult God about it first. It never even crossed our minds. We both had a relationship with Him, but at that time it wasn't at the place where we would go to Him about our plans first. It was more like we would proceed with doing things our way and ask His blessings on it after we'd already begun. In reality, I was forging on with a plan that I did not even know was the right one. It seemed right to me, but obviously my plan was different from God's.

It is a very natural reaction to double down and try even harder to control our situation when things don't go our way. This can manifest in different ways:

1. We can attack our failed plans with a renewed vigor, finding new and different ways to micromanage every detail of trying to bring them to fruition. This gives us a sense that we are in control of the outcome of our efforts.

2. The feeling of our lives being out of control in one area can cause us to become extra controlling in other areas that seem easier to manage. Examples being, the cleanliness of our homes or the behavior of our children or spouse.

This second area is one where we need to be very careful. It is one thing to become more obsessive about how our homes are cleaned or exactly how the laundry is folded and put away. It is quite another to project that need for control onto our spouses and children. This can lead down a negative path quickly, as no one really likes being controlled by someone else. It swiftly inspires resistance. Controlling behavior can also manifest in sneaky ways, so you're not even aware you are doing it.

Hyper criticism and nit-pickiness, regarding little habits around the home or undesirable behavior patterns, will lead to feelings of *angst* in people you're directing that behavior toward. This leads to them either feeling inadequate or angry with you or both, causing conflict between you. Then, not only do you have angst over your plans not working out, you have discord in your home because of the way you are dealing with it. What a mess that can end up being!

It is especially easy to fall into this pattern when we see things getting out of control in the lives of our children. It is so easy to want to step into the situation and try to save the day. When we see them making bad choices and turning down a path that will lead them away from God, it is excruciating to watch. It is almost impossible to let go of our desire to fix things and let God handle it. It is a lot easier to see God's hand at work in the ups and downs of our own lives than to watch it happen in the lives of our children.

I have a good friend I will call Theresa whose son spent years upon years caught in addiction. Alcohol was his first choice, but he used other drugs on top of that. All she wanted as she watched him grow from a precocious boy into a man was for him to find a career, get married, and have a family. Why? Because that was her definition of what a successful life looks like. The American Dream, right?

As Theresa watched him make poor decision after poor decision through his twenties and into his thirties, she despaired of him ever reaching this picture of success. She fell into the trap of comparison. She saw others who filled Facebook with pictures of their beautiful, happy families and grandchildren, and deemed herself a failure as a mother.

She prayed and prayed for years upon years that her son would wise up and get on the right path in life. Never once did she ask God what *His* plan was for her son's life. What *His* definition of success was for her son. She just lived in a state of angst, waiting for God to make her plans for her son come to fruition. I'll share more of her story later.

Sometimes, when our dreams and plans fail, it is relatively easy to pick ourselves up and try again. Other times, we're knocked down so hard and so painfully, it's next to impossible to see how we could do anything other than give up. This was true of a man I once knew, whom I'll call Joe.

Joe met his wife, Michelle, at church. Like many great relationships, they started out as great friends, and then their relationship grew into a passionate love. They married and dreamed of a long life together. They would lie awake together at night, discussing their plans and dreams for the future. Plans to have children, a family dog, places they dreamed of traveling with or without the kids, what they would do someday when they became grandparents and finally retired.

In all the stages of life Joe saw ahead of him, Michelle was right there with him, bringing her light and joy to every moment and milestone. For many years, everything progressed just as they hoped. They had two children, a boy and a girl, got the dog, took family vacations. Then came the day of the cancer diagnosis and everything ground to a halt. Advanced breast cancer, the doctor said. Not caught in time. Prognosis: terminal. Dreams shattered.

How could this happen? What about all their plans? Their young children? How could Joe face the idea of a future without his beloved? The idea of his kids growing up without their mother? Unthinkable. They would fight. They would beat this thing and everything would be okay. God would do a miracle.

Except He didn't. After a long and heroic fight, Michelle went home to be with Jesus. And everything was not okay. Joe was left standing in the wreckage of his hopes and dreams, wondering how he was supposed to carry on alone. Without the joy and life Michelle brought to their home, everything seemed gray and dingy. When he thought of the future now, all he saw was a bleak wasteland of loneliness. How could he be both father and mother to his kids when the light had gone out inside him? Stay tuned for more of Joe's story in the coming chapters.

Some people think following Jesus is supposed to magically mean no problems will come our way and nothing bad will happen to us. They think if bad things do happen, that means God isn't really a good God, or He doesn't love us, or we are not worthy of His love. None of that is true. In fact, the Bible says the exact opposite. Jesus himself said to His disciples in John 16:33, "In this world you will have trouble, but take heart! I have overcome the world." He said this in the context of expressing His great love for them. It is the same for us today.

When we are serving God, He takes all the trials and difficulties in our lives, turns them around, and uses them as part of his plan for us. Romans 8:28 says, "And we know that in all things God works for the good of those who love him, who have been called according to his purpose." Just because things aren't going well now doesn't mean He's not working things for good in your life or that you aren't called to His purpose. In fact, what *seems* like a failure now, is most likely happening for the purpose of that thing none of us like: character development. Distasteful when we're going through it, but so beneficial in the long run.

God uses our pain and disappointments to develop our character and make us more like Jesus, who suffered greatly in His own life here on earth. Jesus was fully submitted to His Father, relying solely on His will and plan in every moment of His life. Jesus was full of compassion for everyone and put the needs of others before His own. God wants us to be like His Son and He uses our trials and failures to refine our hearts, removing the bits of selfishness and pride so we can better be used for His purpose.

God also uses our difficult circumstances to enable us to share our experiences with others going through similar situations in order to bring encouragement to them. 2 Corinthians 1:3-5 says, "Praise be to the God and Father of our Lord Jesus Christ, the Father of compassion and the God of all comfort, who comforts us in all our troubles, so that we can comfort those in any trouble with the comfort we ourselves have received from God. For just as the sufferings of Christ flow over into our lives, so also through Christ our comfort overflows."

When our dreams and plans fail, it creates a myriad of negative emotions inside us. Most prevalent is the powerlessness of being unable to control the circumstances of our lives. The *angst* of finding ourselves stuck in the gap between wanting something and not being able to attain it. When this happens, it is easy to fall into dysfunctional coping mechanisms and try to find ways to feel in control of our lives again. It is also tempting to charge ahead with another attempt at making our dreams happen, which is really just another way of trying to take control. Make sure you consult God and follow His lead before you decide to take that path. It will not only save you a lot of angst in the future, it will also draw you closer to Him now.

DISCUSSION QUESTIONS

1. Are you the type of person who perseveres when your plans fail, or do you get discouraged more easily and give up?

2. Has there been a time in your life where you charged ahead with your own plans without consulting God first? How did that work out for you?

3. Have you ever been guilty of taking out your need for control in your life on those closest to you? What can you do to be more aware of that so you can prevent it in the future?

3

OK, NOW I'M ANGRY

Another way *angst* comes into our lives when our plans and dreams fail, is through the emotion of anger. Anger, in itself, is not necessarily a bad thing. It's a normal part of the grieving process we all go through when something terrible happens. It can, however, turn into a bad thing if we're not careful. Anger can be disbursed in several different directions. It can turn inward, toward ourselves, for failing. A small amount of this can be healthy, in that it can help us see where we can make positive changes going forward. However, too much inwardly focused anger, where we constantly beat ourselves up for perceived failures, can lead to debilitating issues with self-worth and self-confidence.

Our anger can also be focused outwardly toward others who are involved in the pursuit of our dream. This is another area to tread carefully. Relationships with our spouses, children, friends, fellow church members, etc. can be irreparably damaged when high emotions are taken out on others, whether we feel it is deserved or not. Finally, and maybe most commonly, we can direct our anger at God. I have a personal example of this in my own life and the lesson He taught me through it.

After my miscarriage, I was determined to push forward toward my goal of having a family. I was super confident that the next pregnancy would be successful. I had asked God specifically to help us not to get pregnant until it was the right time, so I knew He wouldn't let me down. Over the next several months, we rode the rollercoaster ride that is trying to get pregnant. Our world consisted of ovulation predictor kits, basal body temperature charting, small monthly windows of fertility followed by two weeks of wondering if we were successful, only to be disappointed again and again. It was during that time we learned that trying to get pregnant is not actually all that fun!

After six months of these ups and downs, during which time I confess to becoming increasingly impatient, I found out I was pregnant again. Yay, finally! Huge sigh of relief. We were back on track. We'd failed before, but we'd persevered. Everything would be all right now. The previous setback was behind us, and we were on our way to having the family we so desperately wanted. There was a small amount of fear, now that we'd been initiated into the reality of pregnancy loss, but our feelings were mostly optimistic. This time we were going to have a baby. We were so excited to share the news with our families.

The joy and hope of new life stayed with me for several days until I started spotting again. I immediately feared that I was going to suffer another miscarriage. Jason tried to comfort and encourage me that everything could still be okay, but I was worried. A couple days later, I started having pain in my abdomen and I knew something was wrong. Over the course of that day, the pain migrated to one side and worsened in intensity and I began to suspect I could have a tubal pregnancy.

At the emergency room, I found out I was too early into the pregnancy for an ultrasound to detect whether or not the baby was in the right place. I would have to wait and see my regular doctor in a few days for another ultrasound. To make a long story short, after several different doctor appointments over the course of the next week, it was determined that I did have a tubal pregnancy, and it would need to be terminated immediately to spare my life. Thankfully, it could be done with medicine and not surgery as it had been caught early enough.

To say I was devastated is a gross understatement. My emotions were so conflicted. We'd been on an emotional rollercoaster of hope and disappointment throughout that week until we finally had to accept that this pregnancy was going to fail. I had been so sure things were going to work out this time. My heart was crushed.

For a few weeks as the situation played out, I was consumed with surviving the physical pain I was in. That temporarily distracted me from most of the emotional pain. After a while, however, I could no longer ignore the myriad of feelings going on inside me. Grief, disappointment and disillusionment all coalesced into a fierce anger directed almost exclusively toward God. This was all His fault and I wasn't afraid to tell Him so. Loudly, in fact.

I screamed and cried at Him while rage and anguish swirled inside me like a hurricane, "How could you let this happen? Why?" I had specifically asked Him not to let me lose another baby. I went out of my way to try and submit my plans to Him by acknowledging it may not be the right time for us to have a baby, yet there I was enduring another heartbreaking loss. Bottom line: I prayed and He did not come through. How could He not answer my prayer? I felt utterly betrayed by Him and totally alone. I felt like I could no longer trust Him with the circumstances of my life after He had messed things up so badly.

While I knew logically that God hadn't *made* me lose my baby, in my heart I felt like He'd slapped me in the face by not preventing me from suffering that way. That knowledge didn't stop the ache in my heart or the feelings of abandonment I felt because He hadn't shown up the way I thought He should. I felt like I'd stepped out of the boat expecting Him to help me walk on the water, only to be thrown into the stormy sea to drown.

This began a period of months where I was no longer on speaking terms with God. I felt that He had let me down and I had no desire to talk to Him, much less worship Him. I still believed in Him; I was just so angry I couldn't even stand to be around Him. Even though I still went to church, I would stand there during worship, arms folded over my chest, not singing, internally stewing with rage.

This was my first experience with disillusionment of this magnitude, so I had no grid for dealing with it. Though I didn't realize it fully at that time, God was teaching me some very valuable lessons through that season. Even more so given how extremely difficult and painful it was to learn them. The first lesson was that God does not always protect us from bad things happening in our lives. I needed to learn to accept that—even though I didn't like it. In my mind, He should have answered my prayer, and either let us have a healthy baby or kept us from getting pregnant until it was the right time. He should have protected me from going through the physical pain of a tubal pregnancy and the emotional pain of another miscarried dream. But He didn't, and He had a purpose in allowing things to happen that way, even if it was difficult for me to understand.

The second lesson I learned was that God does not cause bad things to happen to us. He allows them to happen and then uses them to help us grow in maturity and in our relationship with Him. I learned that He was using that horrible experience to build my trust in Him during difficult times. It's easy to trust Him when things are good, but quite another when things go wrong. My first inclination has always been to try and fix my problems myself and then to go Him after exhausting all other avenues. After this, I learned that going to Him first is always the better way because even if things don't turn out the way you hope, there is peace in having Him there with you on the journey. We'll talk more about that a little later.

After a few months of nursing my anger toward God, I began to realize I was acting like a spoiled child who was having a tantrum because she didn't get her way. I felt a little ridiculous for behaving like that. I repented of my anger, entered back into relationship with Him, and our relationship was stronger for enduring the trial.

It may seem like a simple thing to learn to *not* be angry at God for my circumstances, and it's a little embarrassing to admit how immature I was at this point in my life. However, for me, it was a huge lesson that has had a lasting effect throughout the years since. It is common to feel angry when we are confronted with situations where our plans fail, or something bad happens in our lives or the lives of others around us. Things feel out of control and seem unfair, and we want to find someone to blame for what feels like an injustice to us. God is certainly an easy target in times like these. It is important to remember, though, that we see the situation through human eyes with a human's perspective and understanding. God, however, sees with an all-knowing perspective. Isaiah 55:8-11 says:

> For my thoughts are not your thoughts, neither are your ways my ways," declares the Lord. "As the heavens are higher than the earth, so are my ways higher than your ways and my thoughts than your thoughts. As the rain and the snow come down from heaven, and do not return to it without making it bud and flourish, so that it yields seed for the sower and bread for the eater, so is my word that goes out from my mouth: It will not return to me empty, but will accomplish what I desire and achieve the purpose for which I sent it.

This means there is a reason and a purpose for what you are going through—no matter how difficult and senseless it seems. God knows the perfect way and timing in which He wants things to happen in our lives. There is comfort in this if we can work our way through the anger and injustice we feel when things don't happen in our way and on our timetable. God is far more concerned with growing and maturing us to more closely resemble Jesus than He is with our plans and dreams for our lives. He knows how best to bring about the refining our hearts need to be able to live out His plan, and He's not afraid to let us go through some suffering to get us there.

James 1:2-4 says, "Consider it pure joy, my brothers, whenever you face trials of many kinds, because you know that the testing of your faith develops perseverance. Perseverance must finish its work so that you may be mature and complete, not lacking anything." *Joy* here is defined the way you would expect: "cheerfulness, gladness, calm delight."[1]

I'm not sure about you, when I experience trials and setbacks in my life, the feeling of *joy* is not one I consider. In fact, the opposite is true. I feel angry. I get depressed and despondent. I feel sorry for myself and wonder, *Why, God? Why is this happening to me?* The answer to the "why" question is the rest of this verse: because it produces perseverance, which makes us into mature, complete followers of Jesus.

How on earth are we supposed to reach the level of maturity where we enjoy the testing of our faith? First, it is essential to focus on the result of going through the test, and not on the test itself. When you have persevered through trials and are more mature in your character and relationship with God, *that* is something to take joy in. Second, you have to know that your maturity level only increases by persevering through the trials that come in your life. Unfortunately, there is no easy list to check off or steps to work through in order to "level up" on your maturity. It's just grinding it out in the trenches of life's circumstances.

Finally, and most importantly, another way to get to the place of taking joy in trials is to draw ever closer to Jesus. The deeper our relationship with Him, the better able we are to see His perspective on things in our lives, as evidenced in Acts 5:41. The disciples, now fully operating as apostles of the new church, were completely sold out to Jesus and His mission here on earth. They had just seen Him ascend into heaven and had personally experienced being filled with the Holy Spirit on the day of Pentecost. They spread the good news of Jesus and healed people wherever they went. They spent the rest of their time in prayer and fellowship with other believers.

When they were arrested, called before the Sanhedrin, and ultimately flogged for preaching in the name of Jesus, what did they do? Did they weep and feel sorry for themselves? Did they wonder why this was happening? Did they go into hiding out of fear? No! They *rejoiced* that they had been found worthy of suffering for Jesus! Because they had a deep relationship with Jesus, they were on fire for Him and His message, and they weren't surprised to have to go through hardship. Jesus *told* them they would in John 16:33, "In this world you will have trouble. But take heart! I have overcome the world."

Many times, when we go through setbacks and failures, instead of finding joy, we nurse anger and disillusionment because of our circumstances. This will eventually lead to bitterness if we are not careful. The *hurts* of this life provide fertile soil into which the seeds of bitterness are planted. If not removed, it will grow into a bitter root and then a bitter tree that produces bitter fruit.

Hebrews 12:15 says, "See to it that no one misses the grace of God and that no bitter root grows up to cause trouble and defile many." When we are angry at God for allowing things to happen to us, it begins to produce this bitter poison in our hearts. This grieves the Holy Spirit because He doesn't have full access to our hearts anymore. In essence, we've turned away from God in order to turn toward anger and bitterness. This is a form of idolatry. Eventually, this bitterness in our hearts will start to spill out of our mouths.

Jesus says, in Luke 6:45, "The good man brings good things out of the good stored up in his heart, and the evil man brings evil things out of the evil stored up in his heart. *For out of the overflow of his heart his mouth speaks.*" (Emphasis mine) This is a very hard reality to digest. No one wants to think of themselves as evil, and yet it says in Psalm 14:3b, "...there is no one who does good, not even one."

It is not always easy to see when we are bitter about something. We excuse and rationalize our own thoughts. I guarantee we can all think of someone in our own lives who is guilty of bitterness, however, and there is a good chance they'd all deny it to their graves. It's always easier to see bitterness in others than it is in ourselves.

If you are wondering if bitterness has done any stealthy growing in the fertile soil of disappointment in your heart, there are a few things you can do to find out. You can ask a close, trusted friend or family member if they have seen any evidence of bitter fruit in your life or your words. Chances are they have, but possibly not. Sometimes we can successfully hide the evidence of our bitterness behind a falsely positive narrative, for a time. It will, however, find a way to spill out eventually.

I have been guilty of this in my own life. During the months that followed our second pregnancy loss, I would always try to remain positive in conversation with others about it and our hopes for success in the future. Part of me did feel that way, but I was also hiding some ugly feelings inside during my season of blaming God for the emotional pain I was feeling. I felt bitterness and anger that things hadn't happened the way I wanted them to, that other, less-deserving (in my opinion) people were able to have children easily and I wasn't, at the unfairness of life and the fact that I was even having to feel this pain at all.

If this is the case for you, it will take prayer and a revelation from the Holy Spirit to help you identify the bitter root. A way that might help is to go stand in front of a mirror and think about or verbalize situations where you have had hurts, failures, or setbacks. If your face looks like you've just swallowed pure lemon juice, you might be dealing with some bitterness. If anger shows on your face or starts simmering within you at the thought of those things, that is another clue. It will be important in your healing process to repent of those feelings to God and to others in your life that may have been affected by the words of your mouth, so God can help you dig that bitter root out of your heart. Bitterness will steal the joy right out of your life if you let it take hold.

It is a normal part of life to feel anger in response to setbacks, failures, and trials on our path through life. We see things going wrong and demand, "What are you doing, God? Where are you in this situation?" Remember to direct that anger in the proper direction and maintain the correct perspective during those times. God has a plan. He knows what He's doing. He will use the worst-looking circumstances for His glory and your gain in your life, or your loved ones' lives. Draw closer to Him and let your trust in Him grow during those difficult times. Take heart in the fact that He is doing something. He is faithful. Whether we understand it or not, He is at work, and His work will not return void. It will accomplish what He set out to do.

DISCUSSION QUESTIONS

1. Has there been a time when you wrongfully directed your anger towards others following a failure or setback in your life? Have you allowed a bitter root to take hold in your heart?

2. Do you struggle to see any purpose in the setbacks and failures you have experienced along your journey?

3. How can you allow these failures to deepen your relationship with God instead of pushing you away from him?

4

LET'S MAKE A DEAL

Repeated setbacks on the road toward our dreams can be devastating. One is not fun, but surmountable. Two are even worse, but what happens when it's three, four, five times? What if that promotion you've been working so hard to achieve was given to someone else, *again*? What if your marriage is on the rocks *again*, after another good stretch during which you thought, *this time we've finally got it*?

What if your addicted adult child has fallen off the wagon *again*, just when you thought they were doing so well, and this was the time they would finally get their life together? What if the ministry you started because of a word God spoke many years ago has failed *again*, just when you thought that word would finally come to fruition? What if you just wanted to have a darned baby already, but you just kept losing them *again and again*? You want to talk about feeling out of control, well we are really there now!

As for my husband and I? We were still riding that rollercoaster of trying to get pregnant. For me, it had become something of an obsession. I *needed* to succeed at this dream that had become the center of my universe and I felt that need in every fiber of my being. About ten months after my tubal pregnancy, we finally conceived again. Because of the tubal pregnancy, I was supposed to notify my doctor right away when I had a positive home pregnancy test so they could monitor my bloodwork to make sure I didn't have another one. This time, I decided to wait a few days because I'd had a false positive test a few months earlier and I didn't want to jump the gun again.

At this point, our joy at the sight of a positive pregnancy test was severely dampened by the pain of our previous losses. We were starting to get gun-shy. It broke our hearts to share joyful news with our family and friends only to have to tell them a few weeks later that we'd lost the baby. This time only my mom knew, which turned out to be a wise decision.

Three days after the positive test, I started spotting, which started a downward spiral of discouragement and fear. *Here we go again,* I thought. I stayed in bed all that morning because I had the silly thought that not moving much would help the baby stay inside me. But it didn't. Thankfully, because it was so early in the pregnancy, I was spared any physical pain with this loss.

Emotionally, however, was a different story. Part of me was feeling numb to the continual failure of this dream to come to fruition. Kind of growing used to the repeated disappointment. On the other hand, I was really struggling with *why* this kept happening. *Why* couldn't I just have a healthy pregnancy? Was that too much to ask? I needed to know the answer to that question. If I could find a reason why, maybe I could fix it. Maybe I could control it. Anything to alleviate the frustration and *angst* of continually failing at the one thing we most wanted in the world.

This began a stretch of time where I became convinced that I was being punished for something I had done wrong, and that was the reason we kept losing babies. When things feel out of control, we desperately seek to find something we *can* control to achieve some sense of balance and safety in our lives. I guess this was my subconscious way of finding something to control.

I became obsessed with discovering whatever it was I had done wrong and fixing it so we could have a baby. I literally spent hours wracking my brain, going over the sins in my life with a fine-toothed comb, trying to figure out what it might be. I asked for forgiveness for everything I could think of, and then added prayers for everything I couldn't think of as well. I was certain there was something I had done that was causing me to lose these babies, therefore, the solution would be in my control if I could just figure out what it was.

I didn't realize it at the time, but this was a sort of bargaining phase for me. I was essentially saying to God, "Okay, I'll repent of everything I did wrong *if* you will give me a baby. I won't do anything wrong ever again *if* you'll just give me a baby." It is certainly not wrong to repent of sins, but when the motive is to get God to do something for you and not a true heart of repentance, that is a problem. At the time, I felt my heart was genuine, but looking back I see that deep down, my motivation was actually to get what I wanted, not to repent because I was grieved by the sin.

After about a month of obsessing over this, I began to realize how silly it was to think that I could fix or control what was happening based on my past or present behavior. Being a *good girl* wasn't going to help me have a baby any sooner, nor would making a mistake and sinning cause me to lose another one. I realized that in thinking the miscarriages were caused by something I was doing and blaming myself, I was almost trying to act like God myself. I was trying to yank that control away from Him to make me feel like I had a handle on what was happening. I had to learn there were some things I couldn't control no matter what I did, and that was a difficult lesson.

It is normal to want to find ways to *feel in control* when things are getting so out of control. We've already talked a lot about that in previous chapters. What I want to focus on here is the *angst* that comes from thinking our actions and behavior are solely responsible for creating the outcomes of our plans and dreams.

Certainly, our actions play a role, but only to a certain extent. There is much that is still out of our control. For example, you can strive to do your best at work and still not get that promotion. You can change your behavior toward your spouse, and they still may decide to leave the marriage. You may do your very best to raise your child the right way, and they may still make poor choices.

When we see our actions as the sole influencing factor in the success of our dream, it causes us to see the situation from an unhealthy perspective. It is analogous to a child believing their parents divorced because they snuck candy into their room one night after bedtime. Children believe everything is their fault and their actions are the cause of whatever happens around them. This phenomenon is called egocentrism.

Jean Piaget was a psychologist in the 1920's. He formed many of the fundamental theories of child development. He is the originator of the word egocentrism, which is defined in this context as the inability to see things from any perspective but one's own; the belief that we are the center of the universe.

According to Piaget, we are all born naturally egocentric. From the ages of two to seven, we gradually grow to be able to see things from other people's perspectives instead of assuming everyone else sees and thinks as we do. Piaget says as we grow older, we then reach stages of thought and development where egocentrism is no longer a factor.[1]

Much of the research I have done suggests that the prevailing thought of the psychological community is that some people never fully progress beyond the tendency to egocentrism, and indeed most people have areas of thought that are affected by it. This makes sense given that we are all born naturally selfish creatures and have to be taught to behave otherwise.

Bringing this phenomenon into our current situation, egocentrism can cause us to mistakenly believe that everything bad that happens in our world is our responsibility. This is called egocentric guilt.[2] That is not to say we bear no responsibility for things that happen to us, but I am speaking about taking on the burden of responsibility for things that are really out of our control. It can be very emotionally damaging to operate from the place of egocentric guilt. It causes the way we see ourselves to fluctuate according to the circumstances in our lives instead of being firmly rooted in the truth of who we are as a person. We feel good when things are going well, but as soon as they aren't, we go down a spiral of self-recrimination.

There are many ways this kind of thinking can sneak its way into our lives. Do you remember Theresa and her alcoholic son from chapter two? When her son began to demonstrate that he was not going to follow the traditional path to "success" that our society expects, but instead choose the path of addiction and bouncing from job to job and college program to college program, who did she blame? Did she hold her son accountable for his own decisions and mistakes? No. She felt it was her fault (and her husband's as the other half of the parental unit) that he turned out the way he did. It was some flaw in their parenting—a lack of proper discipline or boundaries, or a failure to effectively teach right from wrong. Something. She lived in a state of *angst* for years thinking that way.

What could she have done differently as a mother? Why was her son struggling so much when his siblings were not? She felt like a failure. Finally, she was able to grow to the place where she could rationally see that her son's choices were his own responsibility. She and her husband could have been the most perfect parents in the history of the world and their son could still have made the same choices. He, as his own person, is the only one responsible for his choices. This was a huge lesson for her.

This is a lesson we can learn that will save us a lot of *angst* in our own hearts. There are factors in every situation that are our responsibility: our behavior, our choices, and our thoughts. And there are those that are not: other people's behavior, choices, and thoughts. If your marriage is struggling and you have done all you can do within yourself to save it, and your spouse still leaves, that's on them, not you. If you worked hard and did your very best job and still got passed over for that promotion, that's on your boss, not you. And for me, the fact that I couldn't have a baby no matter what I did, wasn't my responsibility. It was totally out of my control. Every situation has an element that is out of our control. That's just the way the world works. Trying to control and take responsibility for the things that are really out of our control only leads to unnecessary angst.

Let's be honest, most everyone has times when egocentric thinking takes over. Thinking like this is very sneaky. We may not even know we're doing it. It especially manifests itself when we are under duress, and circumstances like those we are discussing certainly fall into that category. No one operates at their best and most rational capacity when they are in the midst of an ongoing and seemingly endless trial. Unless we become aware of it, we can never take steps to change our thinking from egocentric to rational thinking.

Thinking rationally is being able to see things as they truly are, or to see things from all angles and perspectives and see the true cause and effect of things. When we practice thinking rationally, we can begin to realize where our true responsibility and control lies in a given situation and separate it from what is the responsibility of others. This will help our emotions in the face of disappointment to be more stable, instead of oscillating depending on our circumstances.

Learning to retrain our thinking is difficult, but not impossible. Romans 12:2 says we are to "...be transformed by the renewing of our minds." You can create new pathways of thought in your brain that actually change the physical structure of your braincells. In the book, "Who Switched Off My Brain?" by Dr. Caroline Leaf[3], she lays out the scientific research that supports this Bible verse. We really *can* transform our thinking! I highly recommend this book as an adjunct to your internal growth in this area.

Changing our thinking starts with intentional practice. When you catch yourself going down a thought path of egocentric guilt, stop and tell yourself the truth. Own your part of the responsibility and acknowledge that the rest is out of your control. This takes a conscious effort to "Take every thought captive to the obedience of Christ," as Paul says in 2 Corinthians 10:5b. You can also find specific Bible verses that speak to your personal situation and pray them over yourself. Change the wording of the verse into personal pronouns so the verse becomes a prayer of what you want God to accomplish in you.

When we experience repeated disappointment in our lives, it's normal to want to know why. To want to find something about the situation we can fix so we can feel in control again when everything feels out of control. To want to bargain with God to get what you want. This kind of thinking only leads to *angst* when we try to take control of things that are out of our control. Instead, we need to change our thinking toward God's perspective. This effort to renew your mind will be worth the fruit of peace that will bloom in your life.

DISCUSSION QUESTIONS

1. Can you identify any areas where your thinking has been egocentric instead of rational?

2. Have you been guilty of assuming responsibility for the behavior and mistakes of others in your life?

3. How can you begin to be transformed by the renewing of your mind in this area?

5

HOPE DEFERRED

Whew! This whole *angst* business is starting to get pretty rough, isn't it? Maybe even a little depressing? Well, hang in there with me while we slog through this a little longer. I promise we're going to break through to a better place very soon. In order to get where we want to go, we have to make sure we learn everything we're supposed to learn from where we've been. Otherwise, we're doomed to repeat the same mistakes over and over until we do learn.

In Proverbs 13:12 says, "Hope deferred makes the heart sick, but a longing fulfilled is a tree of life." Repeated instances of hope deferred can start to take a toll on our emotional health after a while. There are only so many times a person can get their hopes up about something, only to have them crushed, without completely losing it.

Often, we have to go through bleak seasons of hope deferred in order to make it possible for us to have that vibrant tree of life when we come into the full realization of God's plan for us. Disappointment, grief, and suffering serve as a powerful way to refine our hearts and mature us into the people God intends us to be. Even Jesus had to endure suffering and grief before he came into the fullness of his ministry here on earth. How can we expect God to treat us any differently than He did His own son? He had the wisdom to know that it is the hard times that grow and shape us into a vessel He can use for His plans.

One of the traps we can get caught in when we are continually facing disappointment after disappointment on our journey, is comparing ourselves to others who seem to not be struggling with such issues. This can create a huge amount of angst in our hearts. I fell into this trap on my own journey.

Seven months after our third loss, I had another positive home pregnancy test. This time, I went to the doctor and had my hormone level tested. My initial level was 75, which was low, but as long as it doubled in two days, things could be okay. At this point, I wasn't feeling very confident. I wanted to believe everything could work out this time, but I didn't like the sound of the low hormone level, in spite of the nurse's attempt at reassurance. I was starting to get a bit fatalistic at this point in the journey.

Two days later, I had blood drawn again, and instead of doubling, the level went down. The baby had died. Again. Despondency welled up inside me and spilled out in tears. I was getting tired of riding the emotional rollercoaster of getting my hopes up only to have them dashed on the rocks. My heart was starting to feel like it had gone twelve rounds with Rocky Balboa.

I called Jason to tell him the news and I could hear the discouragement in his voice even as he tried to remain strong and positive for my sake. He said, "Well, I guess we just keep trying." I replied, "To what end? We just keep losing babies. Maybe it's time we saw a doctor for some testing. Maybe they can find a reason why this keeps happening." He agreed and I scheduled the consultation appointment. We tried to remain hopeful, but it was becoming more and more difficult to keep up the effort. We simultaneously feared that the test would show one of us was the problem, and that no issues would be found, and we would be back at square one. As it turned out, after a period of several weeks of testing, nothing could be found to explain our lost babies. I wish almost desperately for a reason, an explanation of *why,* but would have to deal with never having one. I now think that happened on purpose to help me build my faith.

During this season, my every waking thought and prayer was focused on having a baby. I was obsessed. I would find myself looking at other friends or even random strangers who seemed to have no problem at all having a baby and wonder why. Why did they get to experience parenthood and not me? What was so wrong with me that was keeping me from the one thing I most wanted? Would I ever get a chance to be a mother?

I remember a specific time when we were in a small group Bible study with three other couples, all of whom found out they were expecting within a month of each other, right after I had just lost a baby. Seeing those happy, expectant mothers week after week was like having salt rubbed in that raw wound. Not that I begrudged them their happiness, I just wished I could get some too. Jealousy ate at me for a long time and all it did was feed the angst inside me.

Comparison of our lives to others is prevalent in our society. We all do it, if we're honest. We compare the stuff we have, how much money we make, how many activities our kids are in, and the challenges we face. This is especially true in today's age of social media, where all we see of our friends' lives are the perfect pictures they post on Facebook and Instagram.

My friend, Theresa, also fell into this trap with her son. She would see her friends' adult children having successful careers, getting married, and giving them beautiful grandchildren and wonder why. Why did they get to have that, and she had to go through the grief and heartache of a son who was choosing addiction over a "successful" life? Why was God allowing those families to be blessed while her family was going through this hardship? She spent years feeling like she and her family were failing because their situation looked so much worse than others from the outside looking in.

We need to remember that everyone faces challenges that they don't necessarily share with the whole world. Maybe that perfect family you see on social media was only perfect in that one moment and then erupted into conflict after the camera flashed. It may be that the husband is abusive behind closed doors, or one of the two of them are having an affair, or their kids have issues they are hiding from everyone. When we are always focused on what others have that we don't have, materially or relationally, we will operate out of a sense of lack in our own lives. The focus is shifted from how blessed we are in other areas, to the area of deficiency. This leaves us with a constant internal tension because we feel our lives are not measuring up. This is a lie.

People today are not the only ones that fall victim to the practice of comparing themselves to others. There are examples in the Bible of this as well. One that is close to my own heart is that of Hannah. In 1 Samuel chapter one, we read her story. She was one of two wives in her husband's household. The other wife, Peninnah, had many children, while Hannah had not been able to have any. This absolutely tore her heart to shreds. Back then, it was considered a great failure and disgrace to be barren. Children were evidence of God's blessing.

In 1 Samuel 1:6-7 it says, "Because the Lord had closed Hannah's womb, her rival kept provoking her in order to irritate her. This went on year after year. Whenever Hannah went up to the house of the Lord, her rival provoked her until she wept and would not eat."

Not only did Hannah have to have the evidence of her shortcoming in this area in her face every day in her own home, but for years her rival wife was blatantly tormenting her about it on a regular basis. My heart breaks for this woman! She could not live a day without comparing herself to Peninnah, and even though her husband loved her best, she could not be satisfied without a child. For years she lived in a state of angst as she waited to be able to see her dream come to fruition. Thankfully, her story has a happy ending. She finally gave birth to Samuel, who became a prophet of God, and the Lord blessed her with three other sons and two daughters. But she had to go through a great trial to bring forth her own tree of life that was God's prophet, Samuel.

Another person in the Bible who got caught up in comparing himself to others was the apostle Peter. In John 21:15-22, the resurrected Jesus had met the disciples in Galilee after an unsuccessful night of fishing and gave them a miraculous catch of fish. After they shared a meal, Jesus questioned Peter three times about whether he loved Him. He did this because Peter had denied three times that he even knew Jesus on the night before He was crucified.

Jesus was giving Peter the chance to declare his love as many times as he'd denied his Lord, and to recommit himself to following Jesus again. After this Jesus says, "Follow me!" Peter then turned and saw John following them and said, "Lord, what about him?" Jesus answered, "If I want him to remain alive until I return, what is that to you? You must follow me." Instead of focusing on following Jesus down the path He had for his life, Peter was more worried about what John's path was going to be. How well we can relate to this, right?

It's easier to focus on other people's lives than our own sometimes. Jesus gave the solution to this problem right there in His response. "You must follow me." The closer we are to Jesus in intimate relationship, the more focused we are on what He wants us to do from day to day and moment to moment, the less we care what other people are doing on their journey, and the more joy we feel about our own lives.

When we first moved to Rome, GA, I was appalled by the volume of litter I saw along the side of the roads—the backroads in particular, but even main highways. I was not used to this, and it angered me that people could be so entitled and disrespectful as to use nature as their own personal trash can. For months I would stew about it as I drove down the road, even going so far as to go out to pick up trash a few times myself near our neighborhood. It didn't take more than a week before I started seeing it reaccumulating again! What was wrong with people? It was during a long, quiet drive down a litter-infested highway in the midst of my stewing over the trash, that God began to use that trash to teach me three valuable lessons. These lessons came over a period of several weeks. Each one builds on the previous one.

Lesson number one: I could continue picking up the trash on the side of the road forever, and people would just keep throwing more of it out there unless something changed their hearts to care more about their environment. Taking that metaphor into my own life, I could continue to keep trying to pick up the *trash* in my own life—bad behaviors and attitudes—with behavior modification, but unless I *allowed* God to actually change my heart—the root cause of the problem—the trash would keep returning.

Lesson number two: Even in the presence of the trash on the road, I could still go about my life, working and functioning at my proper capacity. To continue the metaphor, I didn't need to wait to function in God's kingdom and do what He wanted me to do with my life until all the *trash* in my life was cleaned up. I can do His work with the presence of trash in my heart, even as He works to heal my heart. This could also be applied to the people around me. I might be tempted to judge, criticize, or be offended by the *trash* they had, or I could love those people even in the presence of their trash.

Lesson number three: If I'm driving down the road and look up at the horizon out in front of me instead of at the road immediately around me, I don't even notice the presence of trash. In my life, that means when look up, I keep my focus on God and the broad picture of where He has me going. Then, I am able to maintain the proper perspective and my *trash* and that of others doesn't matter anymore. The closer I am to Jesus, the more my focus is on Him, the less I care to pay attention to the things I don't have. The less I care to compare myself to others or worry about picking apart their lives, faults, etc. This was a huge lesson for me, and God used litter on the road to teach it to me! Amazing.

We can take much from these lessons about the danger of comparing our lives to others. God has individual plans for each of us, and they are all unique. Your journey isn't supposed to look like your friend's or neighbor's or fellow churchgoer's. It's yours alone, because his purpose for you is unique.

Going through hard times, where things don't appear as perfect as we think they should be, is a reality that most people will face at some point in their lives. No one who is following Jesus closely is immune to struggle. It is His favorite tool to use to refine and develop us into more Christ-like people. Jeremiah 1:5 says, "Before I formed you in the womb, I knew you, before you were born, I set you apart..." He knows what He's doing with your life, even if it doesn't look the same as what He's doing in other people you know. Focus on what He is teaching you even through the seasons of hope deferred and begin to feel peace instead of *angst*.

DISCUSSION QUESTIONS

1. Are you able to look back and see how prolonged seasons of hope deferred have changed and shaped your heart and helped you grow, or are you in the midst of one of those seasons and therefore unable to yet see what growth will come?

2. Have you been guilty of comparing your life and circumstances to those of others around you? How so?

3. How can you take steps to rectify this and begin to shift your focus to gain the proper perspective into your circumstances?

PART II

Awareness

6

THE PIT OF DESPAIR

We have come to a pivotal point in our journey together. A point where we will have to make a choice. A choice to either acknowledge the *angst* we have been creating through our poor coping mechanisms and do something different, or the choice to do nothing and stay in the same place. What exactly are we supposed to do differently, you ask? Don't worry, I'll tell you in the next few chapters.

First, let me share how I reached this pivotal point in my own journey. A year after the last miscarriage, I found out I was pregnant again. In case you have lost count, we are now on the fifth pregnancy. After so many losses, we were struggling to hold out hope that this pregnancy would be a success. I wanted so badly to believe it would, but I have to admit I was emotionally preparing for the worst while trying to hope for the best.

The positive test began a rollercoaster ride that would last over two months. One day our hopes would be high, only to be dashed another day when we received disappointing news from the doctor's office. To summarize as succinctly as possible, I had several blood tests over a period of two weeks that showed a level of pregnancy hormone that was rising, but not doubling every other day as it was supposed to. There was some concern about another ectopic pregnancy. An ultrasound ultimately showed that it wasn't, but the baby did not measure normal growth.

A week later, another ultrasound showed some growth and a heart flutter that was too weak to measure as a true heartbeat. We were elated at first, thinking the news was good. That is, until the doctor came in and told us that by that point in the pregnancy, the baby should be bigger and have a measurable heartbeat. The outlook was grim. It was confusing and upsetting to go from feeling excited and encouraged to disappointment in the span of a few minutes. We scheduled another ultrasound for two weeks later to check the progress.

When that day came, we found that there had been no growth from the last appointment and even the heart flutter was gone. The baby had died. I would have to go home and wait for my body to realize that fact and miscarry or have a surgical procedure to take it out. The rollercoaster had come crashing to the ground, and we were left to pick up the broken pieces of our dreams yet again. As I got dressed alone in the bathroom, I broke down crying. My heart was crushed by the weight of grief and devastation. Pain clawed my insides and my soul screamed in anguish.

I will never forget that afternoon at home after we found out the news that we would be losing another baby. We each called our parents to break the news. When I finished crying with my parents, I went outside and heard Jason talking to his mom. He was sobbing as he told her. It was the first time I had seen him cry throughout all of our losses. He was always the one trying to remain strong and positive for me and seeing him broken like that rocked me to the core. It was the first time I truly realized that this had been hard on his heart too, even though he kept his feelings beneath the surface. That's when I knew in my heart that I was done putting us through all this heartbreak.

It took a week for my body to catch on to the fact that the baby had died and start the miscarriage process. When it finally happened, it was like the first miscarriage only ten times worse because I had been twice as far along. When it was finally over, it was almost a relief to feel my body returning to a more normal hormonal state. Emotionally though, I was a mess. The other losses had been difficult to endure. This one completely broke me.

I felt disillusioned in regard to everything to do with having children. I had lost the desire to ever be pregnant again. In fact, I actively desired to never take the chance of having to go through anything like this ever again. I had reached my breaking point, and I couldn't emotionally handle any more. Jason and I agreed to pursue adoption down the road when we had healed emotionally from the trauma of this experience.

Over the next few months, we settled back into the routine of life, but I was not myself. I had begun to withdraw from living my life. I found myself escaping into everything I possibly could—books, movies, writing, anything to be in someone else's life for a little while instead of my own. I lost interest in doing most anything I used to enjoy, like being active outside or exercising. Instead I would lie in bed or on the couch and just stare at the wall for endless stretches of time. I began to have trouble sleeping, as well. I would lie awake for hours with my mind unable to settle, or wake up after a few hours and be unable to go back to sleep again for several hours. It became a daily struggle just to get out of bed.

There were times where I wished I could just be done with life so I wouldn't have to feel this pain or keep trying to be strong anymore. I would be driving down the road, and thoughts would go through my mind like, *just steer into oncoming traffic or into that tree and it will all be over,* or *just take too many Tylenol and you won't have to deal with this anymore.* I won't lie, it was a very seductive thought, being free from that pain. Only the knowledge that ending my pain would be a source of unspeakable pain for everyone who loved me stopped me from giving in to those thoughts.

During that time, I had virtually no relationship with God. This time it wasn't out of anger, but because it hurt too much whenever I was in His presence. All I would do was cry and cry, so I hid from Him to avoid that.

After several months of wallowing in my misery and barely going through the motions of my life, I began to realize that something was wrong with me. I started to wonder if I was going through depression. Up until that point, I had almost no experience with depression. Of course, I'd had moments or days of feeling down in the dumps or in a bad mood, but nothing that lingered on for months like this or made such a profound impact on my daily life. It was in this pit of despair that I started to become aware that I had a problem with the way I was dealing with things.

Becoming aware of a problem is the first step in overcoming it. That sounds really elementary, but think about it. We can go for days, months, even years without realizing we have a problem in a certain area. We are often as blind to our own personal issues as we are sensitive to problems in other people. It's our human nature.

When there has been a season of hope deferred in our lives, it is very common to deal with depression. It is part of the grieving process. There are two kinds of depression I want to mention here that are similar but not the same. One is situational depression, and the other is clinical depression. "Situational depression is a short-term form of depression that occurs as a result of a traumatic event or change in a person's life."[1] Bad circumstances happen to us and depression can come along with that, causing a myriad of symptoms. Some of these include:

1. Listlessness

2. Feelings of hopelessness

3. Difficulty sleeping

4. Frequent episodes of crying

5. Unfocused anxiety or worry

6. Loss of concentration

7. Withdrawal from normal activities or family and friends

8. Suicidal thoughts

Situational depression is more acute and will typically resolve when one comes to terms with the triggering situation. Talking through and processing feelings with a pastor, licensed counselor or psychologist can be helpful in this process.

Clinical depression is more severe and chronic than situational depression. It is caused by a chemical imbalance in the brain and can be genetic. It doesn't go away when a tough situation is resolved. It is sometimes, but not always, accompanied by other psychiatric symptoms such as delusions, hallucinations, and other psychiatric disturbances. This kind of depression needs a medical diagnosis and a more comprehensive treatment plan than situational depression. Clinical depression can be triggered by difficult situations in life, but it is a chronic condition caused by more than just that situation.

More than likely, most of us dealing with feelings like these would fall into the situational depression category. Mental health is becoming more of an issue in our country. Part of the reason for that, I believe, is the lie we've been fed by society that we have to be super-people and handle everything perfectly and on our own. That, combined with our digital society where everyone has their faces in their phone instead of talking to each other, contribute to feelings of isolation and depression.

We see other people appearing to handle everything in their lives so well and beat ourselves up for not being able to do the same. Well, here's a newsflash for you: we weren't meant to handle it alone. We were created to need a support system consisting of God and a community of other people. Jesus himself says in Matthew 11:28-30, "Come to me all you who are weary and burdened and I will give you rest. Take my yoke upon you and learn from me, for I am gentle and humble in heart, and you will find rest for your souls. For my yoke is easy and my burden is light." He wants us to join up with Him on our journey so that He can relieve us of our heavy burdens.

Another way He uses to relieve us of our burdens is putting us into community with others who can encourage us during our times of struggle. The New Testament is full of references to other believers strengthening and exhorting each other to persevere. An example is in Hebrews 10: 23-25 where is says, "Let us hold unswervingly to the hope we profess, for he who promised is faithful. And let us consider how we may spur one another on toward love and good deeds. Let us not give up meeting together, as some are in the habit of doing, but let us encourage one another—and all the more as you see the Day approaching."

Remember Joe from Chapter 2? He learned this lesson firsthand after his wife, Michelle, lost her battle with cancer. Not only was he reeling from the devastation of losing his beloved wife, floundering in the storm of his own grief and broken dreams, but he had young children who needed him as well. Children dealing with their own grief and pain at the loss of their mother. And he was all alone. Or so he thought.

He fought on for weeks, trying to be strong for his kids, to be both mother and father as best he could, until he reached the end of himself. He tried to rely on God to get him through this season, but he was still fighting to keep his head above water. This was bigger than he could handle alone. He needed help. He needed a friend. He reached out to an old mentor from church who had moved to another state. Joe confessed his struggles to his friend and accepted his invitation for a weekend getaway at his home.

That weekend proved to be a turning point for Joe. He was able to talk about his grief and difficulties with someone who could empathize with his situation. It was a catharsis after weeks of holding everything inside. Weeks of trying to be strong for his kids. God used Joe's friend to speak encouragement into his life, and he was able to return home refreshed and determined not to isolate himself in his grief again.

Don't believe the lie that you have to be strong and get through hard times on your own. Don't give in to the shame that can come with seasons of perceived failure. There will be some resistance if and when you decide to make a change in how you are managing your feelings about your *miscarried dreams* because the enemy of our souls wants nothing more than to keep us isolated and wallowing in shame and misery. Especially if you decide you may want to talk with a counselor about things. Thoughts will come into your mind that say you don't really need help. You can do this on your own. People will laugh at you or think badly of you if you get help.

When I first realized I was dealing with depression, my mind immediately started trying to make me second-guess myself. I convinced myself it wasn't really depression after all—that depression wasn't even a real thing anyway, but an excuse to have a pity party when things didn't go my way. In reality, I was afraid. Afraid to go to a counselor and have them tell me I should be over it already. There was something wrong with me because I was still struggling. I had no right to feel this way for so long after the miscarriage. I should just suck it up and move on with my life. I had so many blessings in my life, so many things to be thankful for, why couldn't I get over the inability to have a child? I thought I would sound like a whiner to them.

Looking back, I see how wrong I was to let that lie keep me from doing something that would have greatly benefitted me and my healing process. Many years later, I got up the nerve to see a counselor. I was motivated to do so for a different reason than my lost babies, but that subject did come up in the course of conversation. She didn't judge me at all for still feeling pain from that. To the contrary, she encouraged me that my feelings were exactly what would be expected from someone who had gone through that kind of repeated loss. So, all my fears were just lies that my mind had told me to keep me from growing and moving on. I encourage you to pay no heed to those voices in your own mind when they try to lie to you.

When we experience painful emotions like these, oftentimes our first instinct is to try to escape the pain. It's too much to deal with and so much easier just to forget about it by doing something to distract ourselves. We can do this in a wide range of ways. There are innocent things like books, movies, games on our phones, social media or more dangerous ones like overeating, alcohol, or drugs. Escaping may seem like a good idea at the time, but in the long run, it is detrimental. Especially if the method of escaping leads to addiction, sin, or broken relationships.

Escaping doesn't bring any resolution to our situation. We experience temporary relief from the pain, only to have it return full force when we come away from the escape. In her book, *The Gifts of Imperfection*, Brene Brown discusses this coping mechanism. She says, "...there is no such thing as selective emotional numbing. There is full spectrum of human emotions and when we numb the dark, we numb the light. While I was 'taking the edge off' of the pain and vulnerability, I was unintentionally dulling my experience of good feelings, like joy."[2]

Instead of escaping into mindless distractions or destructive and potentially dangerous habits, the right thing to do is to turn to God in the midst of our pain. David, described in the Bible as a man after God's own heart, is a great example for us on how to put this into practice. More than anyone else in the Bible, we are given intimate access into his very heart in the Psalms as he continually cries out to God while working through the many difficult situations he faced in his life. It was obvious in his writing that he struggled with depression on many occasions during hard times, and he always turned to God in prayer and worship to get him through it. There almost isn't a single Psalm he wrote that doesn't have some reference to God being his refuge, his strength, his fortress, his deliverer. Psalm 42 is a great example of his struggles with feelings of depression. Verse 5 says, "Why, are you downcast, oh my soul? Why so disturbed within me? Put your hope in God, for I will yet praise him, my Savior and my God."

This is the example we should follow. We should turn toward the pain instead of away from it. That is the way to get through it. Initially, it hurts more to do this, but I have learned the hard way that there has to be some pain first in order to fully heal. It is like the broken bone that has to be set in order to heal properly.

A prophecy about Jesus in Isaiah 61:1 says, "The Spirit of the Sovereign Lord is on me, because the Lord has anointed me to preach good news to the poor. He has sent me to bind up the brokenhearted, to proclaim freedom for the captives and release from darkness for the prisoners." This is the way God intended things to be. We would have struggles in life, and He would be there to help us through them. We would hurt, and He would help us heal. He did not intend for us to try to do it all on our own. It is important for us to become aware of our dysfunctional ways of coping with our hurts and struggles. This awareness allows us to make a choice to handle things differently. When we choose to turn to Jesus and let Him heal our wounds, He transforms us into vessels He can use for His plan and purpose. We just have to humble ourselves and ask Him. We will delve into that more in future chapters.

DISCUSSION QUESTIONS

1. Have you been able to identify any ways in which you are bringing angst into your life after reading Part 1?

2. Have you experienced depression, situational or clinical, on your journey? Were you able to seek help?

3. Have you found yourself guilty of escaping into different activities or habits to avoid your emotional pain? How can you make a change in this area?

7

EVEN IF YOU DON'T

Anyone who has ever dealt with depression will know that the pit of despair is a challenging place to get out of. The thing about depression is that it sucks all the color and joy out of life, leaving you with no energy to do anything at all except lie there and wallow in your melancholy. Ironically, it strips you of your desire to try and get better.

During this phase of my journey, I felt a deep sense of futility inside. I felt like there was nothing I could do to change my circumstances, so why bother doing anything at all? It was so much easier to retreat than to deal with life. I didn't like where I was, but I didn't have the energy or drive to get anywhere else. Feelings like these are incredibly hard to overcome by sheer force of will, and yet that's what it takes to begin to dig yourself out of the pit. The will to be intentional with the choices you are making. The will to seek the Lord and ask for help in doing just that.

It took longer than I care to admit to go from realizing I was dealing with depression to actually doing something about it. I had been so broken by that fifth miscarriage that I just sort of curled up into a metaphorical ball and hunkered down, trying to survive the storm of pain I was feeling. At first, I didn't even realize I had done this, but even when awareness began to dawn, I still felt almost paralyzed. Living was too much work, I thought. This numb survival mode may not be bringing any joy to my life, but the pain was less there. It would be too hard to dig myself out of the quicksand I was in.

Eventually, I came to the place where I realized I would actually be sinning in continuing to wallow the way I was. Knowing full well I had a problem and not doing anything to try and make it better. Let me clarify that statement. It is not a sin to experience depression of any kind. It is either a normal part of grief, a chemical imbalance you can't control, or a combination of the two. My sin was choosing to continue in that state when I knew full-well I could be making an effort to help myself get better and move on. I chose to give in to laziness and fear when I had an opportunity to choose to start moving along the path of my life again. When the Lord convicted me of this, I had a choice to make: keep willfully disobeying, or finally start putting one foot in front of the other again. Thankfully, I chose the latter.

Significant change didn't happen overnight, but it did begin to happen. Little choices, little victories, that built until I started to feel more like myself again. Choices like going outside to walk my dogs instead of sitting around the house, spending time with God instead of escaping into a book or movie, and engaging in relationship with my husband and friends instead of isolating myself. Some other lifestyle changes that can help overcome feelings of depression include, getting regular exercise, eating a well-balanced diet, keeping regular sleeping habits, talking to loved ones, joining a support group, taking up a hobby or leisure activity.[1]

I now struggle with a more clinical form of depression as an unfortunate side effect of all the grief I experienced cumulatively over these years. Because of my genetic predisposition for depression due to family history, all the grief depleted important chemicals in my brain and it never fully recovered. I have to take supplements to help me maintain a balanced emotional state. I share that to say if you think you may be dealing with clinical depression and not just situational, please don't wait to get some help. If you have tried lifestyle changes and counseling and it doesn't seem to be helping you fully get past it, again, please get some help. There is no shame in taking something to balance your brain chemistry. It's no different than a diabetic taking insulin or a nearsighted person wearing eyeglasses to see. In this fallen world, our bodies don't always function properly and sometimes we need help. That is okay.

Another important thing that can help us turn toward God as our refuge during these difficult emotional times instead of pulling away from him, is remembering that Jesus, too, was no stranger to suffering and disappointment. In fact, there are many places in the New Testament that show us His human struggle. He was rejected by a large portion of the Jewish people He came to save, namely the religious leaders of the time, who called Him *crazy* and accused Him of being *demon-possessed* and healing by the power of Satan. His own brothers didn't believe He was the Messiah. His mother and brothers came to take Him away from where He was healing people because they thought He was acting crazy. He was tempted by Satan in the desert for forty days. His beloved cousin, John the Baptist, was murdered by King Herod. All this and more before the more obvious suffering of His death on the cross. Hebrews 4:15 says, "For we do not have a High Priest (Jesus) who is unable to empathize with our weaknesses, but we have one who has been tempted in every way just as we are and yet he did not sin." (Parentheses mine)

In Isaiah 53:3 in the NKJV it says, "He is despised and rejected by men, a man of sorrows and acquainted with grief." I sat pondering this verse one day, part of me searching for and taking comfort in the fact that Jesus could understand my suffering, and another part trying to find some justification for continuing to wallow in my feelings of depression. While I was thinking and praying, I quoted that scripture to Him. He said to me, "Yes, but I still did what I was supposed to do." That really struck my heart. In spite of His feelings of sorrow and grief, Jesus was still able to have such a close relationship with the Father that He didn't sin. He was still able to do everything the Father sent Him here to do. *And,* because He was acquainted with suffering, He was also better able to feel compassion for the people He ministered to, whom were also suffering.

That was really eye-opening for me. Our suffering is never in vain. We don't have to be perfectly fixed in order to be able to effectively do God's work. The more broken we are and the humbler we become, the more He can use us for His plans. He is not some distant god who does not understand what we go through here on earth. *He has felt* it and *can help you heal* from any hurt that happens to you.

The rest of the passage in Isaiah 53: 4-5 says, "Surely He has borne our griefs and carried our sorrows; yet we esteemed Him stricken, smitten by God, and afflicted. But He was wounded for our transgressions, He was bruised for our iniquities; the chastisement for our peace was upon Him, and by His stripes we are healed." (NKJV)

When I finally decided to start truly *living my life again,* I began to realize something monumental. If we were never able to have a family—I would be okay. I wasn't going to give up on the possibility, one way or another, but deep down inside, I finally knew I would be okay if it wasn't meant to be. I wouldn't hate God or spend my life dwelling on it. With this realization, I turned a major corner in my journey. *My life stopped revolving around me* and my need for a child, my feelings of failure for not having one, and I began to find contentment in the moment. Gone was the all-consuming obsession with having a baby. I was able to find things to be thankful for in a childless life, like uninterrupted nights of sleep, vacations, and the ability to be spontaneous. The opportunity for a renewed relationship with my husband. I felt free.

There comes a time through the course of the hills and valleys on the journey toward our dreams where we have to ask ourselves a question: If our dreams never come to fruition in this life, will we love God anyway? This is a daunting question to wrestle with. The tendency is to automatically think, 'of course I would.' But deep down, would you be able to love Him without any resentment, disillusionment, or feeling like He'd let you down if your dreams never happened? Let's face it, it's a whole lot easier to praise and follow Jesus when things are going our way. It's when things start going awry that our devotion is really put to the test. Is our love and praise only conditional? *"Bless me* and then I will *praise you?"* Or can we truly say, "I will praise you whether or not you answer my prayers?"

When I first began the journey to have a baby, I would have answered that question with a hearty "yes" and felt I was being absolutely truthful. However, you've seen that through the trials of pain and disappointment in the losses of our babies, my true heart was revealed. My love for God *was* conditional. When things didn't turn out the way I hoped, I got angry and lashed out at Him instead of trusting His plan.

As I look back on that time, I can't feel shame and condemnation for myself for the way I behaved. I was immature—in life and in my relationship with the Lord. I was a slab of gold mixed into a lot of rocky imperfections that were obscuring my true value. Only through the refining process—heating the gold to melting so the rock and dirt float to the top and are skimmed away, leaving more pure gold than before—can the value of the gold be seen and used for its intended purpose. The same is true for our hearts. Through the crucible of pain and trial, God removes the imperfections from our hearts, leaving us more mature and ready to be used for His purpose and plan.

Coming to the realization that I could and would still love and praise God even if He didn't give me what I wanted in my life was like breaking free of a confining mold. I had grown into a better version of myself. A caterpillar turned into a butterfly within the chrysalis of years of loss and broken dreams. This kind of transformation of character is not limited to me alone. It will happen for you and anyone else who allows God to work in the muck of the pain and disappointments that come in life.

An amazing Biblical example of praising God no matter what is happening in your life are three men named, Shadrach, Meshach, and Abednego. We find their story in Daniel Chapter 3. In short summary, they were Jews exiled to the country of Babylon. King Nebuchadnezzar, the king of Babylon, made a statue of himself and forced everyone to bow down and worship it or face death in the fiery furnace. Shadrach, Meshach, and Abednego refused to break the command of God not to worship anyone but Him and would not bow down and worship the statue.

In Daniel 3:13, King Nebuchadnezzar was enraged that they would not comply with his order and he summoned the three men. In verse 15b, he says, "But if you do not worship it, you will be thrown immediately into a blazing furnace. Then what god will be able to rescue you from my hand?"

In verse 16-18, they reply, "O Nebuchadnezzar, we do not need to defend ourselves before you in this matter. If we are thrown into the blazing furnace, the God we serve is able to save us from it, and he will rescue us from your hand, O king. *But even if he does not*, we want you to know, O king, that we will not serve your gods or worship the image of gold you set up." (Emphasis mine)

Wow! Can you imagine that kind of faith? Even if God didn't answer their prayers and rescue them, they would worship him anyway. The remainder of Daniel Chapter 3 shares the rest of the story, in which Nebuchadnezzar is so furious he orders the furnace heated to seven times hotter than usual. Guards are ordered to bind the men and throw them into the furnace, and when they do, the furnace is so hot the guards are killed. Then what happens? The king and everyone there witness not just Shadrach, Meshach, and Abednego walking around inside the furnace, unbound and perfectly fine, but a fourth man that looks like a son of the gods (in reality, Jesus.) God came through for them in the end and they were saved. But they were willing to serve Him whether He gave them what they wanted or not. Can we do the same?

The tension here is the war between the *way we want or expect things* to be in our minds, and *the way God, in his infinite wisdom, has them planned to be.* Often there is a very uncomfortable gap here. We see an example of this conflict in the apostle Peter in Matthew 16:21-25. Peter had just finished declaring, by the power of the Holy Spirit, that Jesus was the Messiah, whereupon Jesus blessed him and prophesied over him in an amazing way. Jesus then began to tell the disciples that He would have to suffer in Jerusalem, die, and be raised to life on the third day.

Well, Peter didn't like that. That plan didn't align with his expectations of what the Messiah was supposed to do when he came. The Jews erroneously thought that Messiah would come and establish His kingdom right away on earth and save them from the tyranny of Roman rule. Jesus dying did not follow that plan. In verse 22, Peter says, "Never, Lord! This shall never happen to you!"

He was so caught up in what he thought should and would happen with Jesus, that he dared to argue with Him about it! In verse 23, Jesus replies, "Get behind me, Satan! You are a stumbling block to me; you do not have in mind the things of God, but the things of men." Peter wasn't at all focused on what God's actual plan was for how Jesus would save the world, he just cared that it looked how he expected it to. Sound familiar? I know I have certainly acted this way in my own life.

Then, in Matthew 16: 24-25, Jesus says to the disciples, "If anyone would come after me, he must deny himself and take up his cross and follow me. For whoever wants to save his life will lose it, but whoever loses his life for me will find it." He's telling us that to follow Him, we have to give up on our ideas of what should happen in our lives in return for what God's plan is.

If we *lose* our lives as we think they should be, we will *find* a better one in what God has in mind for us. It's the yielding part that is so hard, isn't it? Trusting Him? Why is it so hard? Because our plans are familiar to us. We know them so well, right? They're safe because we know everything about them. We don't know all the details of God's plans for us. He chooses to reveal things to us in little bits and pieces, surprising and even baffling us sometimes. It's a little scary—at least for someone like me who likes to have a roadmap and know what to expect.

There is a funny meme that I've seen online depicting what life seems like sometimes with the Holy Spirit in control. See the picture below.

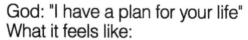

I can completely relate to that picture! I have even considered hanging it on my wall, it speaks to me so much. Often the idea of trusting God through the rollercoaster ride of life when I have no clue what's coming next is absolutely terrifying to me. I know it's not supposed to be. It's supposed to be an exciting adventure, but I was never very adventurous.

So, if you're anything like me and you're becoming aware of your struggle to yield your plans to God, take heart. You are not alone. Remember the words of the popular verse in Jeremiah 29:11, "For I know the plans I have for you," declares the Lord. "Plans to prosper you and not to harm you, plans to give you a hope and a future." Even though it's scary to give up control, you can trust Him with your dreams. Even though it may seem like everything is going horribly wrong, you can learn to praise Him anyway. To say to the Lord, "Even if you don't…I will still serve you."

DISCUSSION QUESTIONS

1. Have you ever experienced a situation where you knew you were supposed to be doing something and/or changing something in your life and you disobeyed God? How did you overcome that?

2. Have you felt like you couldn't be effective in your life's work for God because of your feelings of grief over your lost dreams?

3. Do you struggle to yield control or your plans to God? What can you do to trust him more?

8

STEP ONE: GRIEVE

Now that we have become aware of the angst in our lives as a result of how we are handling our miscarried dreams, it is time to learn how to move away from that *angst* into *acceptance*. We will do that over the next three chapters. I want to be clear that acceptance is not giving up on our dreams and plans and accepting that·they are never going to happen. It's not throwing up our hands and quitting because we've been disappointed one too many times. Acceptance is coming to the place where we realize our dreams won't always happen the way we expect or plan them to *and being okay with that*. It is a place of yielding our plans, dreams, and expectations for our lives or the lives of our loved ones to God. It is accepting that things will happen in His way and in His time, not ours. Peace is found in this place.

The first step in the acceptance process is to *grieve your lost dream*. Grieve the unmet expectations for how you saw things happening. When we have failures and disappointments in our lives, one or many, it can feel like a death to us. The death of our hopes and dreams. I entitled this book *Miscarriage of a Dream* not just because of my story of lost pregnancies, but because of the deaths of dreams we all experience. Because of this, we need to grieve the loss of the dream the same way we would the death of an actual person.

You may have been fighting through the different stages of grief already and not realized it, or you may have been trying to escape and bury such feelings because you didn't think you should be feeling them; that you didn't have a right to feel them. If that's true for you, let me be the first to tell you that it is okay to feel grief over the loss of your dreams. In fact, it is not only okay, but it is necessary and vital to your future emotional health for you to properly grieve. If you escape and bury your feelings of grief, you will never be able to move on to that place of peace and acceptance. You will always be fighting that internal battle of tension and angst that is so mentally, emotionally, and even physically draining.

What does it cost a person to hold back their tears? To cling to the life raft of pride and refuse to show grief? It's as if everything inside you tightens up from the effort exerted to stem the tidal wave that starts in your center and spreads from there. First, comes the lump in the throat. A rising bolus of bitterness that cannot be swallowed away, so that it is a struggle to speak. Then, the chest tightens up like a vice, squeezing tighter and tighter until you cannot catch a breath. The eyes well up against your will so that blinking every second or two is a must. A roaring begins in the ears that would drown out a passing freight train. At the crest of the wave is the head, which seems on the verge of explosion as the skin around it stretches and pulls in protest. And finally, just when you think you will lose the battle, that the tsunami of emotion is too great to stem, it begins to abate. The tension eases, you can breathe again, and you know you have weathered another close call. Pride intact.

Why do people try to hide their pain? Every one of us is feeling it for one reason or another, so why do we think we're alone? Why do we keep it inside and wear a mask so everyone else thinks we're so strong? That we are handling it. That we have it all together, when the truth is deep down, we don't feel as strong as we want everyone to think we are. And we're not handling it at all, but are allowing it to handle us. The dilemma then, is whether or not to reveal this to others and risk judgement, rejection, or just being seen as human instead of the super-people we think we're supposed to be. This was my life.

For some reason, for as long as I can remember, I have internalized pain and hurt instead of finding ways to express it. I am a professional *feeling-stuffer*. When things get hard, my default mode is, "stay strong and get through it." That was how I handled losing our babies. I tried to "move on" like I thought I was supposed to. I didn't think I had a right to grieve for babies that were barely alive long enough to get excited about. I thought I should just get over it already.

The effects of stuffing feelings are sneaky in that they take a long time to manifest themselves. After years of stuffing my feelings of grief over our lost babies, I started feeling the negative effects in my life. I had stuffed so many feelings for so long that I had run out of space, and they started to overflow when I least expected it. I became like a pressure cooker, that can only take so much pressure before it explodes. My feelings started bubbling over onto other people in my life, most especially my husband. Suddenly, every little thing that bothered me had me snapping his head off and losing my temper. Little conflicts and issues in my life that I would normally take in stride, instead had me feeling so stressed I was on the verge of a nervous breakdown. I had no fuse at all. It was just—BAM! Explosion every time. Explosions that caused collateral damage to my husband and others around me. Caused fights with my husband that would not normally have happened.

I'm not saying it's wrong to try to be strong during tough times, but it's a dangerous line to walk. I think a lot of people are this way. Especially in our current society that makes us feel like we need to be super-people that expertly juggle all the many crazy activities in our busy lives. We have to put on a show that we are successfully handling everything, or we feel like we don't measure up.

After a few years of steadily-increasing of conflict in our marriage, my relationship with my husband was in a precarious place. He'd had enough of my volatile emotional reactions to things. Something needed to change, or our relationship would be over. That was a wake-up call for me. It had taken us getting to the verge of divorce for me to realize I needed to do something about this problem.

I knew it was a problem that had gotten too big for me to handle on my own, so I got help. I went to see a counselor, and she made me aware of the fact that stuffing my feelings of grief for years was the root cause of my situation. She taught me how I could change that. One of the most valuable things she showed me was how to release my feelings regularly so my pressure cooker of emotions didn't explode. This was done through journaling, talking to God, and lots and lots of crying. It was hard, and it hurt, but God can't heal what you won't let yourself feel. You have a choice to make, which seems to be a recurring theme throughout this book. Choice. Intention. Taking action. Nothing changes by us just existing. We must choose to move forward or we are actually moving backward. The choice here is to continue as you have been and nothing changes, or grieve, feel the pain, and let God heal it.

Grief is a messy business. It is a very individual process. No two people will handle it exactly the same. It's important to remember this and not compare yourself to anyone else. Everyone will grieve in their own way and time. *The only wrong way to grieve is not to grieve.*

There are stages of the grieving process that have been standardized. They are only meant to be a guide to help you understand what you are feeling and why. They are not absolute. One may progress through the stages as they are listed or go out of order. There is often looping back to stages previously experienced. You may even bounce around from one stage to another in the span of the same day. Everyone is different. *There is no neat progression from one stage to the next.* Grief is all over the place. And there is no time limit, so don't rush it. Don't buy into the lie that says you should be over this already. Grieving takes time, especially if you have been avoiding and stuffing it for any length of time. Allow yourself to fully embrace the process. The five stages of the grieving process are: denial, anger, bargaining, depression, and acceptance. Let's talk about each of these in a little more detail.

DENIAL

Loss causes pain, and we are not ready to face it. Our minds try to compensate for the loss by keeping us in a numb state of shock. After the natural numbness wears off, we may continue to stick our heads in the sand and avoid dealing with our feelings. We may bury ourselves in work or some other form of busyness as a distraction. This stage can go on indefinitely. It is important not to get stuck here by not dealing with your grief. If you don't deal with it now, you'll just have to deal with it later. These feelings don't just disappear. If not dealt with, they can mutate into something worse: bitterness.

ANGER

When the initial shock wears off and we are faced with the pain of our loss, anger is a normal feeling. Anger at the circumstances, God, a person who let you down or passed away, ourselves, whatever. We want to find someone to blame for what has happened. It's normal to feel this way, but it's important to remember not to take this anger out on your loved ones, on other people around you, or even yourself. Find constructive ways to express your feelings without lashing out. (We will discuss this more later on).

BARGAINING

Here we try to find reasons for what happened. We feel guilty. We feel like we could have kept this from happening and try to find things we should have done differently. We try to gain back control of our circumstances by finding ways to fix an unfixable situation. We promise God that if He will just give us what we want, we will do anything, give up anything He wants us to. The bottom line is, we try to find ways to *get around our pain* instead of *going through it.*

DEPRESSION

This is the situational depression we previously discussed. It manifests when we finally give up trying to hide from the reality of our loss and let ourselves feel all of the sadness it brings. Here is where we can fully process all the feelings of loss and pain and where the Lord can do his healing work.

ACCEPTANCE

This is not a magical clearing of the clouds of grief that have been hanging over you. It's more of an acceptance of things as they truly are, not as you wish they were. It's the point where you finally realize that life does go on and can be good despite what you have lost. *A lot of hope can be found in reaching this stage.* Hope for a better future. Hope that God's plans for you will be so much better than your plans ever were. This brings an inner peace as you let go of your attempts to control your situation.

How do you deal practically with your feelings of grief? *Let. It. Out.* You have to get it out of you, or it will eat you alive from the inside. When the painful, sad feelings come, *feel them.* Resist the urge to stuff them down or escape them by finding a distraction to lose yourself in. *Feel the pain* and let it out into a journal. *Feel the pain* and let it out through talking with a good friend, joining a support group, or seeing a counselor. Most importantly, *feel the pain,* pray, and give the pain to God and ask Him to heal it.

This is a very difficult process. There have been times in my own grief where I have sobbed so hard it felt like my body would break apart, but it didn't. I actually felt lighter after I let it out. Like I had been relieved of some of the heavy burden I was carrying. That's what letting it out does. It *unloads the burden.* Let it out in whatever way works best for you, just let it out. *It becomes an emotional cancer if you don't.* And remember to be kind to yourself during this process. Forgive yourself for past mistakes that may or may not have contributed to any setbacks with your dreams and plans. Give yourself grace to grieve so you can heal and move forward.

I've said this before, but it cannot be overstated. Resist the urge to isolate yourself during this grieving process. The enemy of your soul would love nothing more than to keep you isolated from other people who can help you get through this rough time and move on to the better things God has for you. The enemy of your soul doesn't want you to move into the freedom and joy of living God's plan for your life. His sole mission is to keep us from having a close relationship with God and living out our true purpose here on this earth. So, if the enemy can lie to you and keep you stuck in the mire of angst and bitterness over the little deaths your dreams have experienced, all the better. This will ensure that you never reach the place of becoming a threat to him and his agenda here on earth.

John 10:10a says, "The thief comes only to steal, kill, and destroy…" The thief is Satan and he will steal, kill, and destroy anything in our lives that we let him: Peace, relationships, dreams. Satan is like a wolf who goes after a sheep to isolate it from the rest of the flock and pick it off for a tasty meal. He tries to isolate us and then starts planting lies in our minds that keep us stuck in the same ineffective place. But we don't have to let him do this. He only has as much power as we give him. By the blood of Jesus and the authority given to Him after His resurrection, we are not subject to Satan and his lies anymore. James 4:7b says, "Resist the devil and he will flee from you." If you call him out on his lies and tell him to leave you alone in the name of Jesus, he has to obey.

When you're dealing with the tough feelings of grief, you will not want to seek the company of others. However, God works through others to bring comfort to us. He has created us to need the community of others. In Romans 12:15, Paul instructs the church to, "Rejoice with those who rejoice and mourn with those who mourn." God knows us. He knows we need support and compassion during hard times like these.

Jesus showed us an example of this in John, Chapter 11 when He went to Bethany after Lazarus had died. Jesus knew before He traveled there that Lazarus was dead and that He would be bringing him back to life. He told the disciples as much in John 11:11, "After he had said this, he went on to tell them, 'Our friend Lazarus has fallen asleep; but I am going there to wake him up.'"

In verses 33-35, Jesus arrived at Mary and Martha's house and saw how grieved everyone was by Lazarus' death. The Bible says, "When Jesus saw her (Mary) weeping, and the Jews who had come along with her also weeping, he was deeply moved in spirit and troubled. 'Where have you laid him?' he asked. 'Come and see, Lord,' they replied. *Jesus wept.*" (Parentheses and emphasis mine)

He wasn't crying because He was sad about Lazarus' death. Remember, He knew He would be raising him from the dead momentarily. Jesus was moved to tears by His compassion for His grieving friends. This is the compassion we need from our support system during our times of grief—the support we should offer to others as well.

I quoted these verses earlier, but it bears repeating here. "Praise be to the God and Father of our Lord Jesus Christ, the Father of compassion and the God of all comfort, who comforts us in all our troubles, so that we can comfort those in any trouble with the comfort we ourselves have received from God. For just as the sufferings of Christ overflow into our lives, so also through Christ our comfort overflows." (2 Corinthians 1:3-5)

We go through hard times so we can help others through their hard times. This is also true for others who have suffered being able to comfort us during our tough times. If you are currently going through this hard time of grief, seek the comfort of other believers close to you. If you have successfully come through a time like this, be alert and ready to offer comfort to someone close to you.

In order to move beyond the angst that has plagued our lives for so long, we must grieve our lost dreams and plans. There is no way around this step. It cannot be skipped. We will forever remain stuck in the quicksand of stuffing our feelings if we continue to avoid it. It is daunting to release the dam on feelings so long withheld, but it is so worth the effort. It will bring you ever closer to the freedom of acceptance. You can do this. You can be brave enough to grieve.

DISCUSSION QUESTIONS

1. Have you felt like you didn't have the right to grieve over the loss of your dreams and plans? Are you coming to realize that was a lie?

2. Have you been guilty of stuffing your feelings of grief in order to stay strong or avoid dealing with the pain?

3. How will you choose to begin to process and release your feelings of grief?

9

STEP 2: FORGET THE PAST

Now that we have gone through the grieving process over our lost dreams and expectations, it's time for the second step in moving from *angst to acceptance*: Forget the past. I know, I know, another extremely difficult thing to do. But I never said this process was going to be easy. Many people never actually get to the place of acceptance at all because it's just too hard. But I can guarantee it will be worth it when you get through this difficult part and have peace and freedom from the angst you have been living with.

What exactly do I mean by *forgetting the past*? It's not like we can just magically erase unpleasant memories and failures from our minds. In fact, if you're anything like me, it is exactly those memories that are never forgotten. They are often brought out to torment me with their shame when I'm feeling vulnerable and afraid. I'm not saying there is a magic way to forget these unpleasant things from the past. We can, however, get to the place where they no longer have complete control of our lives. Where they have lost their negative power over us. The scar of the wound will always be there, but the wound is healed. It's not merely scabbed over with pus and infection lurking underneath as it was before we dealt with our negative emotions and pain through the grieving process. In order to realize the full potential of the amazing futures

God has in store for us, we have to stop being controlled by past hurts.

Over the years of suppressing the pain in my heart over our lost babies, I exemplified this phenomenon. My heart was deeply wounded every time we lost a baby. With each loss, wound compounded on top of wound, because I didn't allow full healing to occur between each loss. The wounds in my heart would scab over, but there was still *pain* I had not dealt with underneath the scab. Infection, to follow the wound metaphor. Over many years, that infection festered beneath the surface of my heart, injecting poison and affecting my thoughts, feelings, and behavior.

In order for my heart to be fully healed, I had to allow Jesus to lance the infection from my wounded heart. If you think about it, cleaning out an infected wound in our bodies is an extremely painful and ugly process. However, if the infection is allowed to go untreated, it can reach a toxic level in the bloodstream and eventually cause death. The same is true with our heart wounds. If left untreated by Jesus, the infection of *anger, bitterness, and unforgiveness* resulting from our pain will seep into every part of ourselves and can cause spiritual illness—even death.

It is agonizing to allow Jesus to deal with these areas of our hearts. Especially if we've been allowing things to fester for many years. It is, however, the only way we can have hearts that are truly healed of the infection that pain and grief brings if it is left untreated.

An integral step in gaining freedom from past hurts is forgiveness. Forgiveness of ourselves, others we have been wronged by on our journeys, and even forgiveness toward God if we still feel anger toward Him for things that have gone wrong in our lives. Forgiveness is so essential, that we cannot move forward on our journey toward acceptance without it. In Matthew 18: 21-35, Jesus discusses forgiveness in response to a question from Peter, who asked, "How many times must

I forgive my brother or sister who sins against me? Up to seven times?" Jesus replied, "I tell you, not seven times, but seventy-seven times."

Jesus then proceeded to tell the parable of the unmerciful servant, in which a servant owed his master an astronomical amount of money he could never hope to repay in his lifetime. When the master said he was going to sell the servant and his family to pay the debt, the servant begged him for a chance to try to repay it. The master had mercy and cancelled the debt altogether.

The servant then went out and found a fellow servant who owed him a small amount of money and physically assaulted him, demanding that he pay what he owed. When the fellow servant begged for mercy, the first servant refused and had him thrown into prison until he could repay the debt. Some of the other servants saw this and told the master. In Matthew 18:32-35 it says, "Then the master called the servant in. 'You wicked servant,' he said. 'I cancelled all that debt of yours because you begged me to. Shouldn't you have had mercy on your fellow servant just as I had on you?' In his anger, the master handed him over to the jailers to be tortured until he should pay back all he owed. 'This is how my heavenly Father will treat each of you unless you forgive your brother or sister from your heart.'"

Wow. Those are some pretty harsh words. Our Heavenly Father will allow us to be tortured if we walk in unforgive-ness—and not just toward others. We have to include ourselves in this as well. Oftentimes we are harder on ourselves than we are on others, because we have unrealistic expectations of perfection for ourselves, and when we fail, we get mad at ourselves. This is wrong. We don't experience physical torture like the wicked servant did as the penalty for harboring unfor-giveness. Instead, the torture God allows us to experience as a result of unforgiveness is more mental and spiritual.

Who of us hasn't experienced this at some point in our lives? I would wager no one. We relive the negative experience or choice over and over again, feeling all the painful feelings each time as if it was the first time it happened. We agonize over the what-ifs, the should-haves, the if-only's. That's torture. And if it's allowed to go on for long enough, it will lead to bitterness and will even impact your physical health. It is not possible to move forward with healing and fulfilling of God's plan for your life while holding on to unforgiveness. You'll stay stuck in the past forever.

God holds forgiveness in such a place of importance, that in Mark 11:25 Jesus says, "And when you stand praying, if you hold anything against anyone, forgive him, so that your Father in heaven may forgive you your sins." And again, in Matthew 5:23-24 Jesus says it a little differently, "Therefore, if you are offering your gift at the altar and there remember that your brother or sister has something against you, leave your gift there in front of the altar. First go and be reconciled to them; then come and offer your gift." God wants you to forgive and be forgiven even before coming to worship Him! That should tell you how much of a hindrance unforgiveness is.

In Matthew 6:14-15 Jesus says, "For if you forgive men when they sin against you, your heavenly Father will also forgive you. But if you do not forgive men their sins, your Father will not forgive your sins." This issue is obviously very important to God and we should take it equally as seriously as He does.

If you have deep hurts that have been caused by another person's treatment of you, you may be thinking how unreasonable it is that you would be expected to forgive that person. No one can understand what they did, how much they hurt you. There is no way you can possibly forgive them. Let me just say this: Forgiveness is not saying what they did was okay. It is not saying you will ever even talk to them again. What it is, is letting go of the anger and hurt you feel about what they did and giving it to God. It's letting go of the desire to see that person punished for what they did and allowing God to settle the accounts between you in His way and time. It is remembering that since God forgave you all your sins when Jesus died for them, you should not hold someone else's sins against them. Forgiveness frees you from the burden of being controlled by that person, that event that hurt you so deeply and opens up the chance at a future filled with peace instead of bitterness.

You will know that true healing has happened in your heart when you can look back and reflect on past mistakes, failures, hurts, betrayals, etc. and not be filled with a flood of negative emotions like shame, anger, bitterness, and condemnation. When you can look back and see those experiences for the opportunities they were for learning and growing, you are well on your way to acceptance.

Let's take a look at a Biblical example of someone who was able to learn the lesson of *forgetting the past*: the apostle Paul. Many of us know the story of his conversion to Christianity, which happens in Acts 9. I will summarize for our purposes here, but feel free to read it for yourself. Paul, then called Saul, was a very zealous Pharisee. He had big plans for his life. Plans to advance to the furthest ranks of the Pharisees and maybe even become High Priest someday. His passion was fierce. Most of the Pharisees and other religious leaders of that day had refused to believe that Jesus was the promised Messiah. After His resurrection and ascension into heaven, they began to persecute His followers. Saul, in particular, was at the forefront of this persecution, which saw many Christians murdered for their faith in Jesus. He thought he was doing a service to God by doing this. While on his way to Damascus to root out more Christians to persecute, Saul had an encounter with Jesus himself, which radically changed his life. He went from persecuting Christians to preaching Jesus as the Messiah and savior to anyone who would listen.

God totally disrupted Saul's plans with His own, which was for him to be God's chosen instrument to preach His name to the Gentiles and their kings. Saul started going by Paul and spent the rest of his life as a missionary to most of the known world at that time. In many of his letters to the churches he established, he refers to himself as the worst of sinners, saved only by God's grace.

Almost thirty years after his conversion, Paul wrote the book of Philippians, the most joyful book in the Bible. While in prison. He was now a mature Christian, having had many years for Jesus to work in his heart. It is obvious by his writing that he has a deep, intimate relationship with Jesus and has given him full license to change him.

In Philippians 3, Paul speaks of putting no confidence in the flesh, but in Christ alone. He recounts his past fleshly achievements as a Pharisee, only to say that he counts all that as trash compared to the greatness of knowing Jesus. Now instead of fleshly glory, his sole mission in life is to know Christ and the power of his resurrection. In verses 13-15 he says, "Brothers, I do not consider myself yet to have taken hold of it. But one thing I do: *Forgetting what is behind* and straining toward what is ahead, I press on toward the goal to win the prize for which God has called me heavenward in Christ Jesus. All of us who are mature should take such a view of things." (Emphasis mine)

The word he used for forgetting means, "to lose out of mind."[1] It's not that he couldn't remember his past mistakes. On the contrary, he was quick to share them for others to learn from. He just didn't dwell on them in his mind. He put his focus forward, on Jesus, and not backward on his past. In his mind, his mistakes lead him to God's plan for his life. Jesus paid the price for those mistakes, so they were a non-issue for him. He knows his only hope of righteousness is Jesus, so his mistakes are settled in the past. What a place of freedom Paul has found!

This is where God wants to bring all of us if we'll let him. To the place where our past mistakes and failures don't define our present and future. Where we learn from them and use them to help others learn and grow but aren't controlled or defined by them. So many times, we allow our identities to be defined by our actions, whether we succeed or fail, by our own definitions. Our true identity is found in Jesus alone, not in our actions.

When we decide to follow Him and accept His gift of grace and salvation, God adopts us into His family of children. That's who we are. Beloved children of God. (Galatians 3:26) Brothers of Jesus. Co-heirs to the kingdom of God. (Romans 8:17) Not because of our actions, but because of His sacrifice. It doesn't matter what we do or don't do; it won't change God's love for us or who we are in Him. When we truly believe this, deep down in our hearts, it sets us free to be able to live out our true purpose on this earth: to love God and love others.

This is why the enemy will go to such lengths to keep us from knowing our real identities and truly being free from our past mistakes. He uses shame as a weapon to keep us enslaved to the past and fills our minds with lies that God gets mad at us when we don't do what we think we're supposed to do. Lies that our identity is in what we do, not in whose we are.

That is why there is such an identity crisis going on in the world today. People don't want God in their lives. They want to do their own thing, be the masters of their own lives. They don't know their Creator, so their true identities are never found, and confusion sets in, leaving the door open for lies to take the place of truth. They don't know who they are, so they find their identities in what they do. Or they flounder around, dissatisfied with their lives, trying on different identities with none really fitting. That is because we all have a void in our hearts that only God can fill. Nothing else we try to fill it with—hobbies, material possessions, hedonistic lifestyles, relationships, food—will ever work.

Acts 17:28a says, "For in him we live and move and have our being." We are meant to live this life in tandem with Jesus, not try everything on our own and then run to Him when things don't work out. When we do this, we live our lives directed by the Holy Spirit, not by our human nature. Then we don't need to try to fill the void inside us with other things, because it will be filled by the Holy Spirit as it was meant to be. Then we bear the fruits of the Spirit listed in Galatians 5:22-23 of love, joy, peace, patience, kindness, goodness, faithfulness, gentleness and self-control.

In John 15:5 Jesus says, "I am the vine; you are the branches. If a man remains in me and I in him, he will bear much fruit; apart from me you can do nothing." This is the solution to forgetting the past and moving forward with God's plans for you. Remain in Him. We can find the abundant life that Jesus came to give us only when we do this. Then we can know His plans for us and impact the world the way He designed us to. You can't impact anything or anyone to your fullest potential if you are still focused on past mistakes or obsessed with plans you have that are proving to be different from God's plans.

If you struggle as much as I did with seeing yourself the way God sees you instead of seeing yourself through the lens of your mistakes and failures, there are many places in scripture that can help you transform your thinking in this area. I recommend a great devotional called, *Seeing Yourself Through God's Eye*[2]. by June Hunt. It will take you through thirty-one days of scripture to back up your true identity in Christ and was very helpful to me in changing my own thinking about myself. The book *Battlefield of the Mind*[3] by Joyce Meyers is also a great one for learning to combat the lies in our mind about who we are.

To help us put practical application to what we've been talking about here, I'll share another portion of my friend Theresa's story of her addicted son. Throughout the many years of ups and downs she had with him, when she thought that finally this time would be the one where he would get his life on the right track, only to be disappointed again, she kept asking God why. Why was this happening? Why couldn't He just help her son to overcome his issues so he could have a normal life? A job he could keep. A family of his own. Why did He keep allowing all this struggle?

As she continued to cry out year after year, God began to work in her heart and teach her to shift her focus from asking "Why is this happening?" to instead asking "What are you trying to do?" "What do you want me to learn through this?" "What are you trying to accomplish in my son's life that requires him to go through this?" When she started asking these questions, she learned what God was trying to teach her and grew through the trial into a more mature person. She was also able to get on board with praying the right kinds of prayers for her son, because they were more in keeping with God's will and plan instead of praying that his life would magically become "normal."

In order to *forget the past*, or move on from being controlled by our past hurts, we need to take the steps of forgiveness—for others who have hurt us, or ourselves for our mistakes—and changing the focus of our thoughts. Focusing on God and His plans for our future instead of on the past, and asking Him "what" questions instead of "why" questions will continue the process of moving us from *angst* to *acceptance* in our lives. Take some time to draw near to God and find out what He wants you to learn from those past hurts and disappointments, then learn it so you can move beyond the past and into your glorious future in Him.

DISCUSSION QUESTIONS

1. Is there anyone that you are harboring unforgiveness toward in regard to past hurts and mistakes, including yourself? How can you take steps to fix this?

2. Do you struggle with finding your true identity and value in Jesus instead of in your actions and achievements?

3. Are you willing to shift your focus off of asking why and start asking what so you can focus on your future instead of the past?

10

STEP 3: LET GO

We have made it through two difficult steps: grieving our lost dreams and forgetting past mistakes. Now it's time to move to the final step: Let go. It's time to release our grip on the mental picture we have for how our lives, or the lives of our loved ones, should be. Time to accept things as they are now and find contentment. Time to give over control of the future to its rightful owner: God. This might be our most difficult task yet because it involves trust and surrender, two things that are hard enough on their own, but darn near impossible when you've been burned by life's circumstances.

How do you know that everything will work out okay if you yield control to God? How do you know you won't have to go through something painful or disappointing again? You don't. There are no guarantees against hardship in this life, even when we are following God's plans. Stuff happens. It's inevitable that there will be hurts and disappointments, failures and setbacks. Letting go just means that you choose to find contentment no matter what the circumstances. It means you look for the lesson God is teaching you in everything that happens to you and trust that He will bring everything to its proper place in the proper time for His plans. This is a lot easier said than done, that's for sure!

Let's talk about finding contentment in the current circumstances first. In Philippians 4:11b-13 Paul says, "... for I have learned to be content whatever the circumstances. I know what it is to be in need, and I know what it is to have plenty. I have learned the secret of being content in any and every situation, whether well fed or hungry, whether living in plenty or in want. I can do everything through him who gives me strength."

This is no small feat that Paul has accomplished. It is nearly impossible in our humanness to be content when our lives are seemingly falling apart around us, when we are grieved to our very cores and struggling to find answers. When Paul says he's learned the secret of how to do this, we should pay attention. His was not a life of ease. On the contrary, he suffered a great deal in his life, and for him to say he found contentment in all of that is nothing short of a miracle. In 2 Corinthians 11: 24-29, he catalogs what he has suffered:

"Five times I received from the Jews the forty lashes minus one. Three times I was beaten with rods, once I was stoned, three times I was shipwrecked, I spent a night and a day in the open sea, I have been constantly on the move. I have been in danger from rivers, in danger from bandits, in danger from my own countrymen, in danger from Gentiles, in danger in the city, in danger in the country, in danger at sea; and in danger from false brothers. I have labored and toiled and have often gone without sleep; I have known hunger and thirst and have often gone without food; I have been cold and naked. Besides everything else, I face daily the pressure of my concern for all the churches. Who is weak and I do not feel weak? Who is led into sin, and I do not inwardly burn?"

Wow. That's quite enough in itself, but added to this was the shame and guilt Paul felt over his past sins and the rejection of many of his fellow Jews. And through all this, Paul was somehow able to remain content? "Content" is defined as "being satisfied with what one is or has; not wanting more or anything else. Satisfaction."[1]

What is Paul's secret for being able to live in this state? He says it in verse 13, "I can do anything *through him* who gives me strength." (Emphasis mine) It is union with Jesus that enables him to be content and have the strength to weather whatever comes in his life. Without Jesus, this is impossible to accomplish in our own strength.

When we are living in a place of close, deep relationship with Jesus, it is possible to retain peace and contentment no matter what our circumstances are because our peace and satisfaction come from Him, not our circumstances, and He never changes. If we aren't in that place of deep relationship, our circumstances become our focus, and worry sets in, distracting us from the One who is our rock and safe place.

Earlier, in Philippians 4: 6-9, Paul references how we can maintain that peace:

> Do not be anxious about anything, but in everything, by prayer and petition, with thanksgiving, present your requests to God. And the peace of God, which transcends all understanding, will guard your hearts and minds in Christ Jesus. Finally, brothers, whatever is true, whatever is noble, whatever is right, whatever is pure, whatever is lovely, whatever is admirable—if anything is excellent or praiseworthy—think about such things.

Stick close to Jesus and peace and contentment, no matter what your circumstances, truly is possible. This is further supported in Proverbs 19:23 which says, "The fear (loving reverence that includes submission to his lordship) of the Lord leads to life: Then one rests content, untouched by trouble." (Parenthesis mine) This doesn't mean that we won't have trouble or have hard feelings to deal with in regard to that trouble. It means that the trouble doesn't affect our souls when we are in close relationship with the Lord. Just like the old hymn that says,

"When peace like a river attendeth my way,
When sorrows like sea billows roll
Whatever my lot, thou hast taught me to say
It is well, it is well, with my soul."[2]

In both this song and Paul's letter to the Philippians, reference is made to God teaching the person how to be content no matter what. This is an important key. This contentment isn't something that we muster up on our own by positive thinking and willpower. This is something taught and grown in us through the power of the Holy Spirit through time spent in God's presence. That is the secret.

The second part of letting go is the elements of trust and surrender, as I mentioned earlier. Very difficult things to do when we have been disappointed in our lives. It's very important to look intently at the circumstances of our disappointments, however. Often, we pray for things to go a certain way for us or our loved ones, and they don't. Or we have expectations for how God should show up in a given situation, and He doesn't. We are left disappointed, disillusioned, and/or angry because things didn't go the way we wanted them to.

Well, whose fault was that, exactly? God's? Did He actually tell you He was going to do something and then not do it? You hoping and praying for God to do something and Him not doing it, is not Him letting you down. It's your own expectations setting you up for disappointment. That's why it's so dangerous to get ahead of God with our plans and expectations. We can easily set ourselves up for failure. Our only focus should be on what His will is. If we get in tune with that, pray according to that, we will start seeing the answers we want, because we are aligned with His will and not trying to make Him align with ours. When we realize our bad circumstances aren't the result of God letting us down, we can more easily let ourselves trust that He won't let us down in the future.

"Trust" is defined as, "reliance on the integrity, strength, ability, surety of a person or thing; confidence."[3] Proverbs 3:5-6 says, "Trust in the Lord with all your heart and lean not on your own understanding; in all your ways acknowledge Him and He will make your paths straight." The Hebrew word for trust here means, "to hie (hasten; speed; go in haste) for refuge. To be confident or sure- to be bold, secure, put confidence in; to hope."[4]

When we trust God, we put confidence in Him—in who He says He is, and what He says He will or won't do. We rush to Him as our refuge first when things get dicey, not as an afterthought when we've tried everything else. In Hebrews 13:5b-6 it says, "...and be content with what you have, because God has said, 'Never will I leave you; never will I forsake you.' So we say with confidence, 'The Lord is my helper; I will not be afraid. What can man do to me?'" And in Jeremiah 29:11 He promises that His plans for us are, "Plans to proper you and not harm you, plans to give you a hope and a future."

We can trust that even when it may not look like it to us, God is for us and will never leave us. He is always working in every situation, whether we see it or not. When we trust in Him and His promises, we can have the hope and peace we need to feel content in our souls. In Romans 13:15 Paul says, "May the God of hope fill you with all joy and peace as you trust in Him, so that you may overflow with hope by the power of the Holy Spirit."

When we know we can trust God, it makes it easier to surrender control of our lives to Him. He has it anyway. Our sense of control is an illusion we cling to for comfort in times of angst. It stems from fear of the unknown. Fear that something bad will happen, we won't get our needs met, or our hearts will get hurt. I think the fear of pain is something that paralyzes so many of us. We'll do anything to avoid it, and usually the avoidance of it brings more pain in the long run. But what if the most amazing, deep, and lasting lessons we learn in life come through pain? What if some of the most beautiful, poignant, and impactful words we can share with others come through pain? Think about it. Some of the best songs, poems, books, and movies ever created were written by people who suffered greatly in their personal lives. Because pain speaks to pain, and we all have it in this fallen world, whether we try to escape it or not. And the best place for us to seek a deeper, more meaningful relationship with Jesus is in and through our pain.

If we only have a shallow, surface relationship with Him, never letting Him touch the deep places of our hearts, He can't heal us or use us as readily for His greater purpose. It all begins with yielding your pain and need to control your life to Him. When we let go of that illusion of control, we can find comfort and stability in anchoring our hope to the solid foundation of the Lord, our Rock.

"Yield" means "to surrender or submit, as to a superior power."[5] The Greek word for "submit" in the Bible means, "To subordinate; to obey- to put under, to be subject to."[6] When you yield while driving, you stop and allow another car to go before you. You wait on that car before you act with your car. When you yield to God, you let go of your agenda and wait on Him to show you His, then you act based on that. And when He shows you that you need to do something you don't really want to do, you do it anyway. Only He knows how things are going to turn out. Something that sounds totally crazy may end up being the best thing you ever did.

I referenced Matthew 11:28-30 earlier in chapter six when I was discussing how we are meant to live our lives in unity with Jesus. I want to revisit that verse but take it in another direction here. To refresh your memory, Jesus says, "Come to me, all you who are weary and burdened, and I will give you rest. Take my yoke upon you and learn from me, for I am gentle and humble in heart, and you will find rest for your souls. For my yoke is easy and my burden is light."

In chapter 6, I talked about how Jesus wants to yoke up with us to help us bear our burdens. This is true, but in yoking up with Him we are also yielding to Him. The Greek word for "yoke" means "to join; a coupling together; servitude."[7] The dictionary defines it as "to be joined, linked, or united."[8] If two oxen are yoked together, they'd better be united, or they won't get very far pulling their load. They'll spend their journey fighting against each other—each trying to have their way. The oxen also won't get very far if they don't obey their driver. This is what our lives look like when we spend them fighting against Jesus, trying to have our own way.

In this metaphor, the Father is the driver and you and Jesus are the oxen. Jesus always and only did what the Father told Him to do. (John 5:19) We are called to follow that example. When we submit ourselves, our plans, dreams, and loved ones to the Father, Jesus helps us as we carry out what we are supposed to do, through the Holy Spirit. This is living life the way God intended when He created Adam and Eve. Not the way they made it when they decided to take the reins of control away from God and eat the forbidden fruit. They allowed Satan to create doubts in their minds as to whether or not God really had their best interests in mind by not allowing them to eat that fruit. They bought the lie, took control of their own destinies, and every human born since then has been born with the tendency to do the same thing.

Satan is still trying his same old tricks on our minds, trying to place *doubt* there about God's true character and His motives for allowing what He allows. He says things like, "Did God *really* say that?" "You don't *really* need to do that. Do what you want to do. It's your life." Then, before you know it, you've gotten yourself tangled up in the briars on the side of the path God had you walking down, and now you're stuck. Imprisoned. Right where Satan wants you. Right in the place where you'll be virtually ineffective, in your own life and in advancing God's Kingdom.

It goes against our very nature to submit ourselves to God. Our pride wants us to be our own bosses, but the Bible says many times how much God hates pride. Proverbs 16:5 says, "The Lord detests all the proud of heart. Be sure of this: They will not go unpunished." Ouch! James talks about pride as well. James 4:6 says, "But he gives us more grace. That is why Scripture says: 'God opposes the proud but gives grace to the humble.'" James then goes on in verses 7-10 to tell us how do get rid of pride in our hearts. He says, "Submit yourselves, then, to God. Resist the devil, and he will flee from you. Come near to God and he will come near to you. Wash your hands, you sinners, and purify your hearts, you double-minded. Grieve, mourn and wail. Change your laughter to mourning and your joy to gloom. Humble yourselves before the Lord, and he will lift you up."

So, draw near to God. Repent of trying to live your life by your own plan, by your own control, by your own strength, and humbly submit yourself to His direction going forward. Do this and watch and see the fruit that comes to bear in your life.

As we conclude this time spent on becoming aware of the angst in our lives, and the steps we can take to rectify it, it is my sincere hope that you are working through this process in your own heart. I hope that you have and will allow yourself to *feel the pain of your lost dreams* and let it *heal through the grieving process*. I pray that you will stop allowing the hurts and failures of the past to control you, by forgiving those who have wronged you, or forgiving yourself for past mistakes, and turn your focus toward God. Finally, I hope that you will let go of the picture you have of how things should look in your life, and be content with what actually is, by trusting God and surrendering control of your future to Him. This will carry you into the place of acceptance that will allow you to experience true freedom in Christ.

DISCUSSION QUESTIONS

1. Talk about your struggle to find contentment in your difficult circumstances. Were you aware of the secret to attaining this ability?

2. Do you find it difficult to put your full trust in God? Why?

3. Are you willing to surrender your will, dreams, and future to God?

PART III

Acceptance

11

YIELD IT AGAIN

It has been tough to examine our broken dreams and expectations, process our feelings about them, and let them go, but it has been worth the struggle. We are beginning to find *acceptance*. That must mean we're done, right? We're healed, ready to move on to all our dreams coming true? Well, not exactly.

You see, acceptance is not a one-time thing. It's not a place you get to, set up camp, and never think about again. It's a process. A constant, conscious attitude of surrendering to God on a day-by-day, sometimes, minute-by-minute basis. Acceptance can be quite a struggle to maintain sometimes. Your resolve will be tested. Just when you think you've truly let go, something will happen, and you find yourself having to work at letting go *again*. This is a normal part of the process of acceptance.

This happened to me on my own journey to have a family. After that devastating fifth miscarriage, my husband and I disengaged from thoughts of having a family. We just needed a break from the emotional upheaval associated with all of it. Needed time to heal. When I started to pull out of my deep depression, we briefly discussed adoption, but agreed it was best to wait due to the likelihood of us moving to another state sometime in the following year. We didn't want to start the process in one state only to have to start over again in another. It was freeing to be able to release all the mental energy and time I had been spending agonizing over having a baby. When I wasn't wasting all that energy, I almost felt like I could do anything. Weightless even. It was a great feeling.

About twenty months after the fifth miscarriage, we packed up our belongings and our two small dogs and drove from Wisconsin to New Hampshire to begin the next chapter of our lives. It was January, so the drive was treacherous at times, but we were excited for the new beginning.

A month later, after we were finally getting settled in our new home, I found out I was pregnant again. It came as a complete shock because we hadn't been trying at all. In fact, our focus was on starting the adoption process as soon as we were settled in to life in New Hampshire. When I bought the test, I told myself I was being ridiculous to even think I was pregnant because we'd never conceived without trying in any of our other pregnancies, but lo- and-behold the test was positive!

I was completely baffled, my heart racing as I sat in my bathroom staring at the result window, wondering if I was hallucinating. A mix of feelings churned inside my gut. I fought an internal battle between the hope that our change of location would somehow bring about a change in the outcome of this pregnancy, and the ever-present kernel of fear that this would be yet another loss to bear. Finally, I decided to go with hope, shrugged, and said aloud to God, "Well, you know what the plan is, and I don't, so whatever happens I'm okay with it." It was one thing to say that in that moment, but could I maintain that attitude no matter what happened? We would see.

I went to see Jason at work that day because I wanted to tell him, but his parents were visiting, and I didn't want anyone else to know yet. We both felt positive about the outcome of this pregnancy because it had happened without us trying, and we had just begun a new chapter of our lives with the move. Maybe this pregnancy would be the beginning of a new chapter for our family as well.

We were not eligible for medical insurance until Jason had been at his new job for ninety days. This turned out to be a blessing in disguise because I was unable to get my blood drawn every other day as I had with past pregnancies. While I had been grateful for my doctor's careful monitoring of me to rule out another tubal pregnancy, I had not enjoyed the extra stress that came along with it as the numbers failed to rise at the appropriate rate. Now, I was forced to wait and not have any tests done until the insurance kicked in when I would be ten weeks along, by which time we would definitely be able to have an ultrasound done and see right away if everything was going well with the pregnancy. All we had to do was make it until then without going insane worrying!

For a while, it was pretty easy to convince myself that everything was going fine because I started having every pregnancy symptom under the sun, but as my appointment neared, the symptoms started to wane. I tried to tell myself it was just because I was almost at the end of the first trimester, but I wasn't really sure. The familiar feeling of dread had started to take up residence in my belly.

The morning of the ultrasound I was so nervous at work I could barely think straight. It felt like my heart would pound right out of my chest all morning. Finally, it was time for my appointment. It was immediately apparent to me as soon as the doctor began the ultrasound that all was not well. There was no heartbeat, and the baby had only developed to the size of about six weeks, although I was ten weeks pregnant. Obviously, our baby had died, but just to make sure, the doctor ordered a hormone level check to be done that day and then again two days later to verify that the levels were going down and not up. I appreciated the way she handled the situation, but I knew it was over. We agreed that after the blood test confirmed everything, I would have surgery to remove the baby instead of waiting for a painful miscarriage at home this time. I didn't think I could handle going through that again.

When we were alone, Jason hugged me and told me how strong I was. I replied that I was getting tired of having to be so strong. As I sat on the exam table, that's what I felt— tired. Weary of having to bear this grief over and over again. When would it end? While I accepted the circumstances for what they were, I wished I could be free to lose control of myself for a while. Free to yell, scream, and throw things to vent my anger. To tear out my hair and throw myself against the wall to vent my anguish. But I couldn't. I was too strong to give in to those feelings, and the effort was becoming exhausting. And truthfully, I was afraid if I did give full vent to everything I was feeling and lose my self-control, I'd have a nervous breakdown and never be able to find my way back to my normal self again.

Two days passed and the bloodwork confirmed my hormone levels were decreasing, so the surgery was scheduled for the following day. Although I was grieved by the loss of another baby, I honestly felt God's peace with me through the whole process. I didn't struggle with anger this time. I had *accepted* that I had no control over what happened and that *set me free*. This was the first time that I actually still praised Him in the midst of the difficulty we were going through.

Although I was getting better at dealing with my grief, I did deal with some depression over the following months. I struggled with letting go of my pain and giving it to God. I would lie in bed and stare at the wall or cry so hard I thought my chest would rip apart. I could feel the pain and grief clawing to get out of me, yet I was afraid to let it all out. I wasn't sure I could pick up the pieces and be okay again if I did let it all out. I felt almost on the verge of a nervous breakdown. Like I had reached the limit of what I could endure and still stay sane.

It was during this time that God started the process of some deep healing in my heart, and I learned that letting go is a daily decision, sometimes even a multiple-times-a-day decision, not just a one-time thing. It's not enough to decide once to give something to God, and then that's it. Our tendency is to want to pick it back up again and try to take back some control. It's something we have to fight against and continually choose to do the opposite of what our instinct is.

Letting go and trusting God is what sets you free from your life of angst, worry, and tension. From feeling like the responsibility of success in your life or the life of your loved ones depends on your involvement in the situation. This can lift a huge emotional weight from you if you let it. Feelings like those are a prison that keep us from achieving all that God has planned for us. For some of us, letting go can be a big challenge, especially when it involves our loved ones. Sometimes, we find our identities in *helping* them—in always being there for our spouses, children, other relatives and friends with advice, solutions, or financial help.

I placed the emphasis on the word *helping* because sometimes a true desire to help crosses the line into co-dependency if we're not careful. You may think you're helping them, but in reality, you aren't. Especially if the loved one is involved in any kind of addiction. Co-dependency is a situation that develops between two people in a relationship. One of them suffers from an addiction, a chronic mental or physical illness, or some kind of abuse, or is the abuser. Or they are just needy and like being taken care of. The other, is the spouse, parent or other friend or family member of that person. This second person is the co-dependent.

According to Mental Health America, co-dependents:

Have good intentions. They try to take care of a person who is experiencing difficulty, but the caretaking becomes compulsive and defeating. Co-dependents often take on a martyr's role and become 'benefactors' to an individual in need. A wife may cover for her alcoholic husband; a mother may make excuses for her truant child; or a father may 'pull some strings' to keep his child from suffering the consequences of delinquent behavior.

The problem is that these repeated rescue attempts allow the needy individual to continue on a destructive course and to become even more dependent on the unhealthy caretaking of the 'benefactor.' As this reliance increases, the co-dependent develops a sense of reward and satisfaction from 'being needed.' When the caretaking becomes compulsive, the co-dependent feels choiceless and helpless in the relationship, but is unable to break away from the cycle of behavior that causes it. Co-dependents view themselves as victims and are attracted to that same weakness in the love and friendship relationships.[1]

It's okay to want to be there to support our loved ones, but when it crosses the line and we are finding our identity and purpose in that, there is a problem. Things are out of balance. This kind of behavior isn't really helping anyone and is actually dysfunctional. If you feel like this applies to your situation, please seek the help of a professional counselor to help you bring a healthy balance to your life and relationships. Having healthy boundaries doesn't mean that you don't love and support the person you love that is struggling, and to believe otherwise is a lie.

Even if you aren't co-dependent, you may be reluctant to surrender the future of your loved one to God. You may find it extremely difficult to let go of the picture of success you've always had in mind for them, especially if it's your child. Even before they were born, you likely had many hopes and dreams for them. When things don't turn out the way you hoped, it's very difficult. Those dreams don't die easily. You may think you know what their lives should look like better than God does. You might not say that out loud, but the way you think and pray—begging and pleading for things to happen the way you think they should instead of asking His will to be done—would suggest otherwise. Sometimes our children can even become so important to us that they eclipse our relationship with our spouses and even with God. We just love them so much—perhaps too much.

There is an example of this in the Bible with Abraham and his son Isaac. The story is in Genesis 22:1-19. After years of waiting, not always patiently, for the promised son that God would bring them, Sarah finally gave birth to Isaac. Many years later, when Isaac was likely in early adolescence, God spoke to Abraham and said, "Take your son, your only son, Isaac, whom you love, and go to the region of Moriah. Sacrifice him there as a burnt offering on one of the mountains I will tell you about."

God was asking him to sacrifice the son he had waited so long for! The son he loved, possibly more than anything in the world. Maybe because he had waited so long for Isaac, Abraham loved him so much that God felt that he had become an idol to him—something more important to him than God was. The scriptural text doesn't share with us the emotional turmoil Abraham must have felt after God told him to do this, but can you just imagine?

When Isaac was born, Abraham and Sarah had consecrated him to God by the act of circumcision, yielding him and his future to the Lord. Now, God was asking him to put his money where his mouth was and yield him again. This time by sacrificing his very life. The very next morning, Abraham set out to obey. It's worth noting that he didn't put off obeying because it was going to be something difficult. I don't know about you, but oftentimes I put off obeying God right away if He's asking something of me that I really don't want to do. That is rebellion, and it's wrong. Abraham obeys immediately, even though he is being asked to sacrifice the life of his beloved son.

When they reached the place where the sacrifice would take place, Abraham took Isaac away from the servants that had accompanied them and went to build the altar. He told the servants they would be back after they had worshipped the Lord, so it's likely that he was holding out hope that once he sacrificed Isaac, God would raise him from the dead. Even with this hope, he didn't know for sure. Thankfully, once he set Isaac on the altar and raised his knife to slay him, an angel of the Lord called out to stop him. God had been a testing Abraham to see if he would obey and sacrifice the one thing that meant the most to him on earth, his only son. He passed the test, did not have to kill his son, and the Lord provided a ram for sacrifice instead.

Wow. This is the kind of devotion God demands from us. That we yield everything to Him. Everything. Even our most beloved and treasured family members. Even when it looks like He's asking us to sacrifice their very lives, we are to yield. That's a scary thing to do, but you can trust the future of your loved one to God. Even if it doesn't appear so right now, He loves that person even more than you do, and He wants the best for them more than you do. Only He knows what it will take to bring that out in them, and sometimes, it's going through some really hard, ugly stuff.

My friend Theresa learned this firsthand with her son. She fought with herself for years to be able to surrender his future to God. To let go and let God do the work in her son that He needed to do. And it paid off. After the better part of fifteen years of struggling with addiction and all the associated consequences of that, her son finally had a real encounter with Jesus and started to change his life. It was a slow process. Painfully slow at times. Digging out of a deep pit like that always is. But it started happening.

God started planting seeds of truth into her son's heart and it began to grow and bear fruit. His life doesn't look like the picture she always dreamed of for him, but he is following Jesus now and has been delivered of his addiction. God has a plan for him and it is starting to show results. The way and the timing of things happening are not what Theresa would have hoped for, but God knew better what her son needed to go through to develop him into the man of God he needs to be in order to accomplish God's plan for him.

Don't be surprised if your resolve to let go is tested not long after you've decided you're going to do it. It is a certainty that it *will* be tested. God tests all of us to build our faith and prove our devotion to Him. (James 1:3) Remember that letting go and surrendering everything to God is a daily practice, not just a one-time thing.

DISCUSSION QUESTIONS

1. Have you experienced a time where you thought you had surrendered something to God, only to have the issue crop back up again?

2. Do you find it difficult to let go of helping your loved ones? Do you find your identity in being needed by them? Is it possible you have gotten out of balance in this area and are co-dependent?

3. Has God ever asked you to surrender or give up something that you dearly loved to better be able to focus on him? Did you obey?

12

I AM GOD AND YOU ARE NOT

God is God and we are not. We must learn this essential lesson if we are to live our lives from a place of acceptance. When we live our lives trying to be in control, we are essentially trying to be the gods of our own lives. Humanity has been trying to do this since the Garden of Eden when Adam and Eve first sinned, and we are still doing it today. Our natural instinct is to try to take control—to take credit for things in our lives. It's a blow to our pride and ego to accept that we don't have the power to fix or change many things in our lives. We don't know the future, and while there are certain things we can control—namely ourselves and our reactions to circumstances. The rest we really can't control, and trying to only brings *angst*.

There are countless songs throughout Rock n' Roll history that speak to this very thing. The, "It's my life and I'll do what I want when I want" mentality. We think we *know it all*, can *do it all*, and we *don't need* any *help*, thank you very much. Hopefully, you've seen as we have progressed through this book together, how that kind of thinking only leads to *angst*. To fully experience the freedom that God has for us, we need to be able to let Him stay where He belongs in our lives: on the throne as the only sovereign Lord.

We've been talking about yielding and surrendering to God and now we need to talk about why we do that. Because He is the Most High. The Sovereign ruler over all of the universe. What exactly does that mean? The word for sovereign in the Bible comes from the Greek word "despotes," from which we get the word despot. "Despotes" is defined as, "One who possesses supreme authority; Lord; Master."[1] The word despot has negative connotations to us, in that it usually describes a tyrant or oppressive leader of a country, but the dictionary also has the definition, "A king with absolute, unlimited power."[2]

God is not a tyrant or oppressor. On the contrary, He desires nothing more than our freedom, but He most certainly does have **unlimited** and **absolute power**. We would do well to remember and respect that and not take it for granted. He created everything in the known universe and likely many things that are unknown to us. From the great vastness of space to the intricate balance of cellular functions within our bodies. Every system works perfectly together to keep things working in proper order. Amazing!

Our tendency is to put God in our little boxes and reduce Him to a manageable size because it makes us feel more comfortable and less afraid of the unknown aspects of His power. The problem with that is He is a big God, and He could never fit into any box. Remember the passage I quoted earlier from Isaiah 55:8-9 that says, "'For my thoughts are not your thoughts, neither are your ways my ways,' declares the Lord. 'As the heavens are higher than the earth, so are my ways higher than your ways and my thoughts than your thoughts.'" We could never hope to think or operate on a level anywhere near God's level of intelligence and power. We shouldn't even try.

The story of Job is a great example of this. The entire book, found in the Old Testament, tells the story of a season in Job's life that is the stuff of nightmares. For those of you not familiar with this story, I will summarize it. In the first two chapters, we are introduced to Job, a righteous man who revered the Lord and whom the Lord had richly blessed. He had seven sons and three daughters, thousands of cattle of various kinds, and many servants. He was the greatest man in his area of the world.

In the beginning of the book, we are allowed to see a scene from the very throne room of Yahweh (the Hebrew covenant name for God.) One day Satan came to present himself before the Lord, and God drew his attention to Job. God boasted of Job's righteousness and Satan retorted that the only reason Job served God was because God had placed a hedge of protection and blessing around him. If all that were taken away, Job would surely curse God's name.

God allowed Satan to test Job, and in one day, all his livestock was either killed or stolen, and his children all died when the house they were in was destroyed in a tornado. Can you imagine the devastation Job must have felt? To lose one's worldly wealth and means of support is scary enough, but to lose all ten of your beloved children at once? And yet he did not curse God for his troubles. In fact, in Job 1:21, he knelt down in worship in the midst of his grief over the deaths of his children and said, "Naked I came from my mother's womb, and naked I will depart. The Lord gave and the Lord has taken away; may the name of the Lord be praised." Wow. This guy is my hero! I sure didn't have that attitude when my children died.

In Job chapter two, we return to the throne room, where Satan is back in God's presence. God again drew attention to Job, pointing out how righteous he was even after losing everything he had. Satan retorted that staying righteous after losing his possessions in one thing, but if God were to strike out against his flesh, Job would surely curse him. God agreed to allow Satan to attack Job's health, but not to the point of death. (This illustrates how Satan's actions are limited by what God will allow him to do.)

Satan went out and struck Job with a horrible disease that caused painful sores from the soles of his feet to the top of his head. He was miserable. His own wife came to him in

Job 2:9-10, and encouraged him, "Curse God and die!" Yet he replied, "You are talking like a foolish woman. Shall we accept good from God and not trouble?" Wow, again. I want to be like Job when I grow up!

The next several chapters show Job's friends coming to be with him in his time of trouble. That was helpful for a time, but then they all started speculating on why all this was happening to him, and that became a real trial for Job. The main theory they had was that Job had somehow sinned and was being punished, to which Job adamantly replied that he had done no such thing. Even back then people had the mistaken idea that bad things only happened to bad people as punishment for sin. If bad things happened to good people it could only mean that God was not really good, or that He was not powerful enough to stop it. That is a lie.

Being privy to scenes from the heavenly throne room, we know without a doubt that Job was not being punished for any evil behavior. He was God's most faithful servant, after all. And yet God not only allowed those trials in his life, He drew Satan's attention to Job Himself. It's not as if Satan went before God asking to smite Job. God pointed Job out to him!

Why would He do that? What was He thinking? It's likely that God was thinking that as righteous as Job was, he still had some character development and refining that needed to be done in his heart, and this was the way God was going to accomplish it. This is further evidence that God is more concerned with our character than our happiness and comfort.

While Job does not sin by cursing God for his troubles, he does spend most of the rest of the book complaining about how God has dealt with him considering how righteous and moral his life has been. Sound familiar? Does this sound similar to how we behave when things go wrong for us? I know I'm guilty of complaining to God when things don't go my way.

At the end of the book of Job, God himself finally responds to Job's rantings. In Chapter 38: 1-5, He says:

Who is this that darkens my council with words without knowledge? Brace yourself like a man; I will question you, and you shall answer me. Where were you when I laid the earth's foundation? Tell me if you understand. Who marked off its dimensions? Surely you know!

God then spends the rest of chapters 38-41, not answering Job's questions as to why all these bad things happened to him but pointing out His own sovereignty and divine power. In chapter 40:2 He says, "Will the one who contends with the Almighty correct him? Let him who accuses God answer him!"

Job replied, "I am unworthy- how can I reply to you? I put my hand over my mouth. I spoke once, but I have no answer- twice, but I will say no more."

Then God said in verses 8-14, "Would you discredit my justice? Would you condemn me to justify yourself? Do you have an arm like God's, and can your voice thunder like his? Then adorn yourself with glory and splendor, clothe yourself in honor and majesty. Unleash the fury of your wrath, look at every proud man and bring him low, look at every proud man and humble him, crush the wicked where they stand. Bury them all in the dust together; shroud their faces in the grave. Then I myself will admit to you that your own right hand can save you."

Wow. What can you really say to that? Putting things in their true perspective, none of us was present with God when He formed the earth. None of us has the power to create the vastness of the stars and planets in the universe, the plants and animals of the earth, and all the minute details that make it function and hold everything together. What power He has! Who are we to question Him? To question His motives and methods of operation in our lives? In short, we are nothing, and yet He loves us enough to send His Son to die in our place so He can have a relationship with us. There are no words.

Job said in response to this in chapter 42:2-6, "I know that you can do all things; no plan of yours can be thwarted. You asked, 'Who is this that obscures my counsel without knowledge?' Surely I spoke of things I did not understand, things too wonderful for me to know. You said, 'Listen now and I will speak; I will question you, and you shall answer me.' My ears had heard of you but now my eyes have seen you. Therefore, I despise myself and repent in dust and ashes."

Job finally got it. No matter what happened in his life, good or bad, God was still God. He was always in control, always working with a purpose. Just because we can't understand it, doesn't make it any less true. His ways are higher than our ways. After Job learned that lesson, his relationship with God was stronger than ever before, and God blessed him with twice as much as he had lost during this trial, including more children.

So, whether we like it or not, think it's fair or not, God allows His beloved children (us) to go through hard times in life to grow our character. He is the author of the stories of our lives, each of which make up the greater story of humanity as a whole. The most compelling books and movies have characters that seem to lose everything, but go through an amazing, redemptive journey and end up doing great things. How could we expect God, the first and best author of all, to do anything other than make compelling stories of our lives?

Think about this, if you reached the fulfillment of your dreams before the time is right, you wouldn't be ready to handle it and would likely fail in some way. This long process of growing and maturing your character through trials will get you ready for what's to come with your dreams by the time you get there. Trust God through the process. Remember, He can see the big picture of everything that's going to happen throughout the whole rest of your life and everyone else's in the world. All you can see is the little picture of one day at a time. He knows best and He is for you.

Romans 8: 31-32 says, "What then shall we say in response to this? If God is for us, who can be against us? He who did not spare his own Son, but gave him up for us all- how will he not also, along with him, graciously give us all things?" He is not holding out on you. He is growing you into the person you need to be to be able to handle the fullness of His plans for your life. He is God and you are not. And that's okay.

DISCUSSION QUESTIONS

1. Do you have trouble allowing God to sit in his rightful place on the throne of your life? Why?

2. How do you think you would handle things if you lost everything that mattered to you in your life the way Job did? Would you still be able to praise God or would you get mad and curse him?

3. Are you beginning to see how God is using the circumstances of your life to grow and mature you to become more like Jesus so you can fulfill his plans for your life? How do you feel about that? Does it help you to have a better perspective on the hardship you have endured?

13

A NEW DREAM

Now that we have let go of our obsession with our making old dreams and plans happen in our way and time, we can look toward our futures and embrace the new ones God will put in our hearts. Sometimes these new dreams and plans will resemble your old dream but will look a little different. The timing might even be different than you thought. Other times, the new dream will be something you never thought of before, that will suddenly become a new passion. I have experience with both of these scenarios. In regard to my journey through infertility, it was the first one. I eventually received my dream but it looked vastly different than what I had originally planned.

After my sixth miscarriage, we started to look into adopting a domestic infant, meaning one that came from inside the United States. We found a law firm in California that showed promise in matching couples with birthmothers more expediently than we'd found in other places. We spent the next several months saving money for the large deposit that was required to get the process started. By the time we reached our goal and it was time to pull the trigger, we both agreed we didn't have a good feeling about the whole thing. So, we backed off from that and decided to regroup and try another avenue of adoption.

Not long after that, we had another couple over for dinner. They knew of our struggles and we shared our recent decisions about adoption with them. Then, the woman, whom I'll call Jane, dropped a bombshell on us. She said God had laid our situation on her heart over the last few months, and she felt called to offer to carry a baby for us as a surrogate, or gestational carrier as they now call it. We were so stunned we didn't know what to say! We had wished for something like this, but never really thought too much about it because it seemed unrealistic. To have her offer to do this was such an amazing miracle. The seeds of hope that had lain dormant for so long in our hearts sprang back to life. The four of us agreed to take time to think and pray about it and meet again in a couple weeks.

When we met again, none of us had any bad feelings about going forward with Jane being a gestational carrier for us. We agreed to start the process, and if anything happened along the way that was a red flag, we would know it wasn't the right thing to do. I set up an appointment with our reproductive endocrinologist as soon as we could get in, which was about a month from then, so there was nothing more we could do until then but wait and pray.

The day before our appointment, something very curious happened. I had been very sick with a bad cold and bronchitis and hadn't paid much attention to my monthly cycle. I felt crampy and thought my period would start soon, but a few days passed without any sign of it, so I decided to take a pregnancy test. Usually, whenever I thought I was "late," taking a test just to make sure would ensure that my period would show up that very day. I never for one second thought it would be anything but negative. I was wrong. The window said "pregnant."

I remember laughing in disbelief and asking God, "What are you doing?" The irony of the situation was just hilarious to me. There I was, less than twenty-four hours away from our appointment to pursue surrogacy, which we believed God was orchestrating, and I was finding out I was pregnant! Sometimes I just have to laugh at God's sense of humor. He must get such a kick out of watching us make our plans, knowing the outcome is going to be so much different than we think.

Jason and I had been arguing earlier day, so there was some lingering tension between us when he came home from work. In spite of that, I knew I needed to tell him the news right away. When he came into our kitchen, our conversation went something like this:

"So, I found out something interesting today," I said.

"Oh yeah? What is it?"

"I'm pregnant." I wish I could have taken a picture of his face at that moment because the look of surprise on it was absolutely priceless.

"What?" he asked.

"I know," I agreed and handed him the test stick, which I'd been carrying in my pocket for just this moment.

"How can you be pregnant?"

"It must be immaculate conception," I joked. (I had been sleeping in the guest bedroom for what seemed like weeks because of my horrible cough.)

"What about our appointment tomorrow?"

"I think we should go and get the information about surrogacy and not tell him until the end that I'm pregnant. I mean, let's face it, the odds are not exactly in our favor here. This way when we lose this one, we'll at least be able to start the surrogacy right away."

So, that's what we did. We learned about surrogacy and then told the doctor our news. He laughed along with us about the irony of the situation and ordered a hormone level test to be done that day and again two days later. A large part of me was not at all excited to be on this roller coaster ride another time—one I had never intended to ride again.

When the nurse called with the results the next day, I was so nervous I felt nauseated. All the times I'd ever had this test done the first level had always been pretty low. Like, below 100. So, my expectations weren't very high that this time would be any different. When she told me the level was 1409, I was floored. That was the highest it had ever been at only four and a half weeks. For a moment I almost felt hopeful that this pregnancy would be different, but I didn't want to get ahead of myself.

They drew blood again the next day in the hopes that the hormone level would double from the last test, showing healthy growth. In all our pregnancies this had never happened, so when the nurse called and told me the level was now 3425, I was blown away. That was more than double! We were off to the best start we'd ever had and we both felt like we were living in a parallel universe—one where babies didn't always die. Things like this just didn't happen to us. The nurse scheduled an ultrasound for a week and half later to determine if there was a heartbeat, another thing we'd never seen before, and we settled down to wait and try not to go crazy in the process.

That week and a half felt like a year as time crawled by. We told Jane and her husband about things, just to be up front, and they were as anxious as we were about the results. My feelings vacillated, sometimes moment by moment, from trying to be positive and hopeful to trying to steel myself against the worst happening yet again. I tried distracting myself to keep my mind off it with limited success. I studied pictures online of what a normal six-week ultrasound should look like so I would be able to tell right away when our ultrasound started if things were okay instead of waiting for the operator to tell us. The night before our appointment I barely slept; my mind was racing so fast. I kept praying for the strength to handle whatever happened.

Thankfully, our appointment was first thing in the morning, so we didn't have to wait long after waking up. A good thing, since I felt on the verge of a panic attack by the time we got to the doctor's office. I felt my heartbeat in every inch of my body. I could not keep still as my body vibrated with nerves while we waited to be called back. I was sure I would jump out of my skin any minute.

When the nurse finally called us back, I froze. I almost couldn't do it. I wanted to know so badly, but at the same time I was completely terrified. What if it was bad news? As long as I didn't know for sure, there was still a flame of hope burning inside me. I didn't want to lose that. But I had to go. The moment of truth had arrived and there was nowhere to hide.

I got on the table and the nurse started the ultrasound. Because of my research, I could tell right away it was good news. The baby looked like it was supposed to, and I could see the heart beating. Relief surged through me and I was finally able to take a deep breath and relax enough to enjoy this peek at our baby. The nurse turned up the volume and we heard the beautiful sound of our baby's heart beating strong and sure at 115 beats per minute. The first time we'd ever heard one of our children's hearts beating. We were both so overcome with joy that it overflowed into tears. Our baby was alive!

The nurse gave me a due date of November 29, 2009, snapped us a couple of pictures to take home, and we were done. Not even ten minutes had passed, but my world was totally rocked. It felt surreal. We might actually be having a baby this time! We scheduled another ultrasound for two weeks later and walked out into the bright morning sunshine, a reflection of the joy and hope shining inside of us. We looked at each other, both wearing huge grins of disbelief. We didn't even know what to say to each other, what to think. We were so used to getting bad news, we almost didn't know how to handle good news. We just kept saying, "It's alive!" over and over again. We agreed to tell our parents and Jane the good news, but no one else until after the next appointment. Then, we got in our cars, and went to work, our hearts much lighter than they had been half an hour before.

The emotional high from finding out our baby was alive carried me through a week and a half before I started to worry again. For a while, it was easier for me to keep my mind off it since I knew that the baby was alive. Or at least it had been. What if something had changed? Was everything still okay? I wanted to believe all was well, but as the appointment drew closer, the voice of fear whispered inside me that things could change. We could still lose this baby. There were no guarantees.

The last few days before our appointment seemed to take as long as the previous week and a half put together, but it finally arrived. My nerves were considerably less pronounced this time, but butterflies were still fluttering in my stomach. When the ultrasound began, I could tell right away my fears were unfounded. There had been obvious growth from the last time, and we could see the heart beating right away. I was amazed to see the baby had little arm and leg buds, and we were both sure we saw it move! We were given a couple pictures to take home and another appointment for two weeks later, and away we went. It was starting to look like we might actually be having a baby this time!

By the time our next appointment came, I was starting to feel pretty yucky—nausea, fatigue, mood swings, etc. I just kept telling myself the worse I felt, the better it probably was for the baby because it meant it was growing. When the ultrasound began, we could see there had been growth since the last time. The baby measured the right size for ten weeks and had a strong heartbeat again. We could definitely see it moving this time, though I couldn't feel it yet. We were released from the specialist's office to my regular obstetrician with joy and wishes for a happy, healthy pregnancy.

It was great news, but the bad news was we would no longer be able to check in on our baby every two weeks. Our next ultrasound wouldn't be until eighteen to twenty-two weeks, when we could find out the gender. It was then that my fears transitioned from the pregnancy failing, to the more normal fear that we were actually having a baby, and I would undoubtedly screw it up somehow. After all we'd been through, what if I wasn't a good mother? This time I would finally get the chance to find out.

The rest of the pregnancy passed mostly normally and uneventfully. I was so excited to find out if we were having a boy or girl, I almost couldn't stand it. I truly didn't care one way or the other. I just wanted to be able to plan how to decorate the baby's room and start buying clothes that weren't gender-neutral. My husband would've been happy with either as well, but wanted a boy just a little more than a girl because he is the last male in his family that can pass down the family name.

On the day of the ultrasound appointment, I joked with the technician that I wasn't going to leave until she told me if it was a boy or girl, even if I had to stand on my head. Thankfully, the baby cooperated, and we found out we were having a boy. We exchanged silly grins again, and I think Jason got a little misty-eyed. It was so fun for me to be able to think of our baby as more of a real person now that we knew its gender. It was an extra special moment for Jason, being able to tell his father the good news that the family name would continue another generation. It meant a lot to Jason to be able to give his dad that gift.

On December 1, 2009 at 11:35 am, after twelve and a half hours of labor, we welcomed Caden Avery into the world. Our miracle! Our seventh baby—God's number of completion. It was a difficult labor, with over four hours of pushing, but seeing his beautiful face as the doctor laid him on my chest made all the hard work, all the pain of our previous losses worth every minute.

He was so perfect, this little blessing from God, and I was completely overwhelmed, in the most wonderful sense of the word. Of course, he looked just like his daddy, but isn't that the way it goes? It's hard to fully describe the overflow of emotions I felt in that moment. I was almost delirious with exhaustion from the labor, but Jason and I were both half laughing, half crying as we met our son for the first time. The culmination of seven years of gut-wrenching struggle and grief now turned to joy at the fulfillment of our dreams. Even as I write this, a lump of emotion clogs my throat and tears fill my eyes just remembering that day. God is so good!

My dream of having a child looked much different than I originally planned. Instead of having three kids before age thirty, I was having my first live one at age thirty, and he will likely be the only one, considering he is now ten and we haven't yet had the blessing of a second miracle. However, this dream was still a beautiful one, even though it was different. Being an older mother gave me much more patience and maturity than I would've had at twenty-three, which has been a much-needed asset given the fact that our little miracle turned out to be a very strong-willed child. God knew exactly what He was doing when He gave us our child at just the right time in our lives. Caden is full of such personality and love of life that it just sparkles out of his beautiful, blue eyes. He has brought such incredible joy to our lives. He truly is a miracle.

I haven't given up hope that maybe someday God's plan for our family will include another miracle. However, Jason and I said to each other the day Caden was born that if he was all we were ever given, it was more than we ever dreamed of having after all our losses, and we would be content with that. And we are. It doesn't erase the pain of the other losses or change the fact that I will always miss my other children. Always wonder if they are boys or girls and what their personalities are like. I will always look forward to the day I get to meet them in Heaven. Reaching the fulfillment of a dream doesn't remove the pain you went through to get there but going through the pain sure makes it that much sweeter when your dreams come true.

* * *

I have also experienced the second scenario where God puts a totally new dream in your heart that you never would have imagined. That dream for me is being an author. I was never much of a writer growing up. I always loved to read, but writing was never something I thought much about doing until after my fifth miscarriage. During my period of depression, when I was finding any and every way to escape that I possibly could, I became obsessed with a popular TV show. So obsessed, in fact, that I would spend hours on the online message boards for the show.

It was there that I discovered a glorious thing called fan fiction. For those of you who don't know what that is, it's where fans of popular books, shows, movies, etc. can take the characters they have come to love and write their own stories with them and post them for others to read online. I got sucked into reading other people's stories on the message board, until one day I was inspired to write one of my own. I ended up writing several after that, one of which was long enough to be a full-length novel by the time I was done.

I got halfway through the sequel for that one when I began to feel convicted about how much time I was devoting to it. It had become an addiction to me—escaping like that. An idol. I wish I could say I obeyed that conviction and stopped right away, but I didn't. After some time and an increasing sense of guilt, I did finally stop writing the fan fiction. The love of writing had been awakened inside me, however, and I began to write stories with characters of my own. It's amazing how God can use even something as silly as fan fiction to awaken a dream I never realized was inside me. He has given me ideas for many books now, including this one, and I am excited to see where He will lead me in the future as I pursue this dream of writing.

My friend, Joe, was also able to find a totally new dream. In the months following Michelle's passing, he not only grieved the loss of her presence in his and his children's lives, he grieved the loss of the future they'd planned together. Growing old now seemed a bleak prospect instead of a fun adventure to be experienced with the love of his life. His heart ached over the death of the future he'd envisioned.

He threw himself into the daily routine of working and caring for his kids. Eventually, he began to reconnect with friends and fellow church members he'd distanced himself from initially. He felt God beginning to heal his heart. Mornings began with a spark of hope instead of tears and the dread of slogging through another day without Michelle. And then it happened. The day he knew in his heart he was going to be okay. He would always miss Michelle, of course, but he was going to be able to live without her. Not just survive, but truly live.

Not long after this realization, God brought a new woman into Joe's life. At first, he balked at the thought of allowing someone into his heart again. What if he took a chance on love and tragedy struck again? Could he survive that a second time? Could his children? Was it worth the risk? The battle raged inside him—faith or fear? Accept the gift God was offering him—not a replacement for Michelle, but a new future with a new person. A new dream. Or give in to fear and deny himself and his kids the chance at a different kind of joy. Eventually, Joe decided the new dream was worth the risk, and he married this new woman. They are now living out their new future together.

Maybe you will experience both of these scenarios in your life—your dream coming true but looking very different than you thought, or a totally new dream—or only one. Only God knows. Maybe the job you have your eye on and just can't get isn't happening because you're not ready and you'll get there eventually, or maybe God has an even better job lined up. It's possible that He's growing you in your current job until the time is right for the new one. Or, perhaps He'll plant an entrepreneurial dream in your heart and you'll be drawn down that path in the future.

Maybe that marriage you think is failing now isn't really failing. Maybe God is using this challenging time to work through some deep issues inside both of you, and He will eventually restore it. Maybe your child will never have the "perfect" life with the six-figure job, spouse, 2.5 kids, and a dog. Maybe success for them is simply that they are following Jesus at all. Maybe His plan for them will include a family at a later date than you hoped, or maybe it won't.

Maybe God will heal your terminally ill loved one and you can give Him the glory for a miracle. Maybe He won't and you'll have to endure a time of grief before He reveals a new dream to you for your future. Maybe the ministry you've always had in your heart will come to fruition in a totally different way and time than you thought it would. And maybe the picture will change and sharpen into focus in a totally new way that will bring greater fulfillment to you and glory to Him than you ever imagined possible.

Whatever scenario it ends up being for you—a different version of your original dream or totally new dream—enjoy the *process* of getting there. Life is lived in the journey as much, if not more, than in the actual realization of our dreams. Don't miss out on the daily joys you could be experiencing because your focus is too far ahead or lagging behind on things that are out of your control. Take life day by day. Pray for God's will to be done in your life and watch and see what He will do.

DISCUSSION QUESTIONS

1. Are you ready to embrace either a different version of your original dream or a totally new dream altogether?

2. Have you experienced either of these scenarios already in your life?

3. Is fear trying to keep you from embracing this new future, or are you learning to trust God more fully?

14

FREEDOM

We are nearing the end of our journey together. If you have allowed God to work in your heart throughout the process of reading this book, you may be starting to feel something strange—a lightness of heart and mind as you let go of the burden of trying to control your circumstances. This strange feeling is called freedom. Living life in a state of acceptance instead of angst brings freedom.

True freedom is not something that many people experience in our society. You might wonder what I mean by that. Do we not, here in America, live in a free country? Yes, we live in a country where we have personal liberty, but that isn't the kind of freedom I'm talking about. I'm talking about emotional and spiritual freedom. A state in which we live as God intended for us to live—fully surrendered to Him, engaging in an intimate, daily relationship with Him. This allows us to operate without worry or burden for the present or future, living securely in each moment of our day knowing we are totally loved and accepted by our Heavenly Father.

From this fully connected place, we can more accurately and intimately know what His plans are for us. Then, as we encounter the people God wants us to impact for Him, we are ready and in place. We also have the added benefit of the increased joy, spiritual sensitivity, and improved interpersonal relationships that this connected living produces.

I don't know many people who live in this place. Do you? To be honest, I haven't fully arrived there yet myself. Oh, I've had seasons of getting pretty close, but have allowed the busyness of life to pull me off course. Our society certainly isn't conducive to living this way. It's very much like swimming upstream in a world where we are bombarded with angst, worry, fear, negativity, strife and outright lies every time we turn around. This happens thousands of times a day via news, social media, and even in our circle of family and friends. It is difficult, if not impossible, to fight against all of that and remain positive and sane.

It's no wonder that mental health in America is suffering. That anxiety disorders are through the roof. That people you thought were stable are suddenly snapping and shooting up their workplaces or taking their own lives. A person can only handle so much of this bombardment without some sort of release or support before they snap. In our increasingly isolated society, that just isn't happening. The best support system we have at our disposal is a close relationship with Jesus. When we are reminded daily of His sovereignty and divine perspective on things, which sees the whole picture at once instead of our limited perspectives, we can more easily surrender any worries that come. Without that, it's only a matter of time before some kind of breakdown happens.

God did not create us to live in a constant state of angst. Our fallen world has produced the angst we now live in, but it wasn't originally like that. When God created the earth and everything in it, He said that it was good. He put Adam in the Garden of Eden and gave him dominion over the animals of the earth and every plant for food. In Genesis 2:15-17 it says, "The Lord God took the man and put him in the Garden of Eden to work it and take care of it. And the Lord God commanded the man, 'You are free to eat from any tree in the garden; but you must not eat from the tree of the knowledge of good and evil, for when you eat of it you will surely die.'"

One of the first things God says to Adam, before Eve was even created, was "You are free..." What does that even mean? To be free? The dictionary defines freedom as, "The state of being at liberty rather than in confinement or under physical restraint; exemption from external control, interference, regulation, etc.; the power to determine action without restraint."[1] Our society would tell us it means being able to do whatever you want whenever you want without consequence or regard for what anyone else thinks. That's a lie. The Bible talks a lot about freedom and it has a much different picture to paint. That picture shows us that when we do what we want, when we want, we are not free, but actually putting ourselves in bondage because we are living for ourselves instead of God.

Right after God tells Adam he is free, He immediately also creates a boundary for him to stay within. Adam is free to do anything *except* eat from one tree. Why does God do that? Isn't imposing a boundary denying Adam true freedom? On the contrary, it is only within this boundary that Adam can experience true freedom. God put that boundary there for Adam and Eve's protection. Before they ate from that tree, they were innocent. Free from sin. They didn't even know there was such a thing as good or evil or sin. They were like little children before they learn the harsh reality that life is not always good. Because of that innocence, they were able to be in the tangible presence of God as He came to walk with them every evening in the cool of the day.

He knew if they ate from that tree, they would be aware, as He was, of the existence of good and evil. Except without His omniscience and unfathomable wisdom, they would be unable to handle that knowledge. They would be tempted to act as their own gods because they would think they knew everything. If you are a parent, you will recognize this protective action. We do this with our own children, don't we? We establish boundaries in our homes for their protection, and to preserve their innocence. When they step outside those boundaries, consequences happen. God does the same with us.

As we know, Adam and Eve stepped outside the boundary God set for them and ate from the forbidden tree. And what happened? They lost their freedom. The ultimate consequence of sin was that it put them, and the rest of humanity after them, in bondage to sin. One minute they were free and innocent, enjoying the garden and the close, intimate relationship with God they had access to because of that innocence. The next minute it was all taken away. Their innocence was lost, they knew they were naked and vulnerable, and shame entered the world. The chains of bondage were slapped on them, and they got kicked out of paradise and were forced to toil and slave to grow food from the land. And, worst of all, their relationship with God was drastically altered because they were no longer able to be in His direct presence without dying, because of their sin. A pretty drastic consequence for one bad choice.

Why did they do that—make that bad choice? God was pretty clear about His plan for their lives, right? They were to be one with each other, make babies, and take care of the Garden of Eden. Pretty good plan. They felt safe and secure in their knowledge of their purpose, in their knowledge of God and their daily relationship with Him. Until the devil came and tempted them to question that safety and security. Up to that point, Adam and Eve were living their lives fully surrendered to God's plan.

Genesis 3 tells us what happens next. In verse 1, Satan says to Eve, "Did God really say, 'You must not eat from any tree in the garden?'" He starts by making her question what God said, and also twisting and misquoting what God actually did say. When Eve replies, she also misquotes what God said to them.

In verse 3, she says, "…but God did say, 'You must not eat fruit from the tree that is in the middle of the garden, *and you must not touch it*, or you will surely die.'" (Italics mine)

Eve added the italicized part to what God originally said. Now Satan has misquoted God's instructions and Eve has also. He's got her confused, and then he goes in for the kill. In verse 4 he says, "You will not surely die. For God knows that when you eat of it your eyes will be opened, and you will be like God, knowing good and evil."

Satan confused Eve as to what God actually said, then he called God a liar and caused her to question God's motive for forbidding them to eat the fruit in the first place. He got Eve to think that it was possible God was keeping something from them—something amazing—by not letting them eat that fruit. Maybe God didn't have their best interests at heart after all. Why else wouldn't He want them to be like Him? Eve began to feel afraid, insecure, because the safety and security of her position in God was being questioned, and she was tempted to take control of her circumstances. Fear lead to pride. Pride told her that maybe God didn't know best, maybe *she* knew better, and she chose rebellion against God's plan, destroying her freedom in the process. The Bible also says Adam was right there with her and didn't even speak up during any this.

Does this sound familiar? Haven't we all experienced this? We feel like God has placed something in our hearts to do—follow a certain career path, write a book, start a ministry, go back to school, have a child, the list goes on. We feel confident in that plan until things start to get tough. Until an obstacle arises. Until the voice in our heads—the devil or our own selves—starts to question if we really heard God correctly about the plan. If it were God's plan, surely there wouldn't be obstacles, right? The fact that there are must mean this couldn't possibly be the right path after all. So, we get scared, insecure, and start questioning if God is really *for* us—if He really knows what He's doing.

We buy the lie that being in God's will isn't a safe and secure place to be—and fear creeps in. Our fear reduces Him from a big, capable, good God down to a more limited, potentially fallible God and we don't feel safe in His hands. Then pride comes in and tells us that we know better. Our way seems to make more sense, and it's easier or faster—insert your own rationale here. We take control, do our own thing, make our own plan, and end up losing our freedom. Just like Adam and Eve.

I personally have had this very thing happen to me in the process of writing this book, and I'm ashamed to say that I have let myself get thrown off track more than once. In fact, even as I write this, I am coming out of a season of defeat that started when it was time for me to write these last chapters on freedom. I was consistently writing a chapter a week for a few months. Then I got to the topic of freedom and—bam!—my life exploded and I had no time to write. I slipped into an emotional funk so that even when I did have time to write, I was unable to find my voice. I ended up wasting four months of my life in bondage to the fear that I could not possibly write about freedom when I was so pathetic at living it out in my own life.

Then I was reminded that the struggles we face and over-come are often used to help encourage others going through similar experiences. I was reminded that I am a *work in progress* just like everyone else in this world, and I don't have to have everything mastered in order to help encourage others on their own journeys. God can and will use an imperfect vessel to proclaim His message of freedom to the world.

If we're going to live in freedom, we first have to stop believing the lies we've either told ourselves about ourselves, or the lies we've allowed the enemy to whisper in our ears our whole lives. Or both. These are not lies that only a few fall victim to. They are lies that are common to all people.

We've already seen that the enemy has been lying to humanity since the first two were created. We need to recog-nize these lies for what they are and refuse to allow ourselves to believe them anymore. Lies about God that say He is not good. He doesn't care about you individually. He isn't looking out for your best interests. He's not for you. Following His plan is settling for less, and you'll be missing out on something if you do. Lies about you that say you're not good enough, brave enough, smart enough, charismatic enough, or equipped enough to accomplish what God has planned for your life. Lies that you'll fail or look and sound stupid. People will laugh at you, get angry at you, feel betrayed by you if you move forward with God's plans.

What about the fact that you've been disappointed so many times along the way? Why should this time be any different? How do you know you won't be disappointed again? Fail again? The answer is, you don't. That's where faith comes in. And what you see as a failure and a disappointment, God sees as an opportunity for you to learn, grow and mature into the person He wants you to be. The person you need to be in order to do what you need to do.

If you reach the full success of your dreams before the time is right, before you're developed enough through the tough school of life experience, you won't be ready to handle it and you'll eventually fail. The long process of growing and maturing your character through trials will get you ready for what's to come by the time you get there. So, start viewing those disappointments and apparent failures the way God does—as opportunities. Ask Him what He wants you to learn from them. Stop letting your fear and insecurity about your future hold you prisoner. Allow God to replace the lies you have believed for so long, with Biblical truths. Then you are on your way toward freedom. Then you are on your way to pursuing your dreams the way God wants you to—with Him in the lead, not you.

DISCUSSION QUESTIONS

1. Are you starting to feel lighter of heart as you have moved through the process of healing the hurts of past disappointments? Share specifically what you are feeling.

2. Do you identify with making poor choices and disobeying God's plan because of fear, pride, and rebellion? Share an example of a time when this has happened to you.

3. Identify and share some of the lies you have been believing about God and yourself that have held you back from experiencing true freedom in your life.

15

FREEDOM AIN'T FREE

God's original plan for humanity was foiled when Adam and Eve decided to take the course of their lives into their own hands and disobey Him. That disobedience placed them, and all humanity thereafter, into the bondage of sin. What would God do about that hopeless situation? How would He fix that mistake and set us free from the bondage of sin? He had a plan to provide a Savior. Enter Jesus.

We owe a debt to God that we can never repay. A debt of sin that we have no power to wash away, atone for, or eradicate. But Jesus can. Jesus came to earth, willingly limiting Himself to being confined in a human body, to be the perfect atoning sacrifice, thereby purchasing our debt of sin from God with His blood and His life. He did this so we could have an opportunity for freedom again. That is seriously good news! But the story doesn't end there. We play a part in the process.

First, we have to accept the gift Jesus gave us by taking the death sentence for our sins upon Himself. That's salvation. Then, we have to fully surrender ourselves to His lordship, giving our lives, our wills, over to Him. The old, sinful us has to die in order that Jesus might live in and through us. Because He died for us, purchasing our debt of sin from God, we give our lives to Him in return. He then lives through us, accomplishing more for the glory of God than we ever could on our own.

Paul says in 2 Corinthians 5:15, "And he died for all, that those who live should no longer live for themselves, but for him who died for them and was raised again." And in Galatians 2:20 he says, "I have been crucified with Christ and I no longer live, but Christ lives in me." Paul was talking about his "self," or his will to serve himself, that had to be crucified so that Jesus could fully live in and through him and accomplish His great plans in Paul's life. And what plans they turned out to be! All it cost Paul was his own agenda for his life.

The process of surrendering ourselves to the lordship of Christ so He can heal and renew us for His glory is called sanctification. This process takes a lot of time to complete because there are many of areas in our lives and hearts to surrender to Him. Some of them are easy to let go of, and some we cling to with a death grip. It's also a very difficult process, because our "self" doesn't die easily. It has a strong sense of self-preservation, if you will, which is helped along by the enemy.

If you are involved in something that God wants you to surrender to Him, and you don't obey, you've given Satan a weak spot he can exploit in your life. Even if what you're supposed to let go of isn't something that is obviously a sin. It's a part of your life that you are in bondage over because you become a slave to whatever it is you won't let go of. For example, it could be a physical activity such as eating, drinking, reading, playing games on your phone, and so on. Anything that has gotten out of balance and started to come before God in our lives. God demands to be first in our lives, so if anything has started to become more important than Him in our lives, the Holy Spirit will bring conviction in order to bring things back into balance. Reading is not a sin, but if it's a major priority in your life over God and other more important things, it becomes an idol and therefore a sin. Mental and emotional strongholds such as worry, fear, perfectionism, and self-limiting lies and beliefs are further examples of areas we give ground to the enemy.

Some people never make it very far in the process of sanctification. They've accepted Christ's gift of salvation, but they don't want to surrender their lives to Him in return. Because of that, they may have been a Christian for a long time, going to church regularly or not, but their lives don't really reflect very much of Jesus. In order to be more like Jesus, we have be less like our natural selves. If we don't surrender our lives to Him, even those difficult areas, He won't be able to accomplish much in sanctifying our hearts.

Some of us have more of these areas than others, but we all have them. One I have always struggled with personally is trying to do things in my own way, strength, and timing. That's pride. What is at the root of that pride? Fear. Fear that God doesn't have my life under control, even when things look bad to me. Fear of hoping for something good in my life only to be disappointed again and again. I try to make myself feel less anxious by controlling things, and in doing so put myself in bondage to the enemy. I have learned to surrender things to God's control, but that is not a one-time decision. If I'm not doing that on a regular basis, every single time something comes up that I could choose to get anxious about, I can fall right back into bondage all over again. This has unfortunately happened many times. It is an issue in my life that I just keep circling around, thinking I have overcome, only to deal with it again.

Another big one for me is distractions. Things that are not necessarily bad in and of themselves, but end up getting put before spending time with God or on what He has given me to do. Distractions like reading, social media, games on my phone, etc. You may identify with some of my issues, or for you it may be something different. You may be holding on to unforgiveness, lust, an addiction to something, your finances, and the list goes on. We are called to surrender all of these things to the Lord.

Matthew 16:24-25 says, "Then Jesus said to his disciples, 'If anyone would come after me, he must deny himself and take up his cross and follow me. For whoever wants to save his life will lose it, but whoever loses his life for me will find it.'" He talks about this again in John 12: 23-25 when he says, "The hour has come for the Son of Man to be glorified. I tell you the truth, unless a kernel of wheat falls to the ground and dies, it remains only a single seed. But if it dies, it produces many seeds. The man who loves his life will lose it, while the man who hates his life in this world will keep it for eternal life."

Jesus isn't talking about the literal losing of our life, although that is something we could possibly be called to surrender at some point. He is talking about us giving up on our own ideas and plans for our lives. If we cling to our stubborn wants and ways of doing things, we will lose out on the life He has planned for us. If we, instead, give our lives to Him, fully surrendering every part of ourselves, our plans, and dreams, we will find the abundant lives He wants for us. If we "die" to our will and surrender to His will, we will be able to produce many seeds for His kingdom and glory instead of just being one seed.

When we finally surrender everything to Jesus, even those really tough things in our lives, we will be free from the bondage the sin of living for our "self" places us into. Then we can say as Jesus did in John 14:30b, "...for the prince of this world is coming. *He has no hold on me*, but the world must know that I love the Father and that I do exactly what my Father has commanded me." (Emphasis mine)

The prince of this world, or Satan, had no hold on Jesus because Jesus was without sin. He was "self"-less. Jesus died to give us the opportunity to have that freedom as well. But we have to be careful we don't get it only to lose it again. In Galatians 5:1, Paul says, "It is for freedom that Christ has set us free. Stand firm, then, and do not let yourselves be burdened again by the yolk of slavery."

Freedom is ultimately a choice we have to make to let go of whatever we are stubbornly clinging to that is holding us back from it. We have to get sick enough of living like that so we can let it go and exchange it for something much better. And then don't go back to it ever again. That can be a problem, can't it? We think we've left some old habit or problem behind, but find ourselves slipping back into old ways after a while, usually when something bad or stressful happens in our lives.

Let's face it, freedom can be scary sometimes. Putting trust in someone else instead of ourselves is new and unknown. It can feel safer and more comforting to be in those old places of bondage because at least they're familiar. We know what to expect from that life. Sometimes we even do this to ourselves on purpose, at least on a subconscious level. We get going on a good path toward freedom. We're feeling good, doing what we need to do, and then things change. Life gets crazy and we stop spending time with God regularly. We get scared. Scared we don't really know where we're going, and when we get there, we won't have what it takes to be able to do what God wants us to do anyway. So, we self-sabotage and end up right back where we started.

This has happened to me a couple times while writing this book. I'm scared to finish it and then have to move on to what comes next with publishing, marketing, speaking, etc., which is much more difficult for me than the writing. That fear has sent me on a couple of downward spirals into old, bad habits. Perhaps you're experiencing something similar in your own life: an opportunity to go into business for yourself that you know you should take, but fear is holding you back. Or, a relationship you're in that you know isn't right for you, but you don't want to be alone, and you're afraid nothing better will come along. A ministry you have on your heart to start, but don't feel fully equipped for. The list goes on.

It takes constant surrender to God—daily, even hourly, or minute-to-minute if necessary, to keep us from slipping back into bondage again. As soon as we stop doing that, the slow fade begins. The slow fade from freedom back into bondage. If we are not moving ever forward toward God and freedom, we are sliding backward into old ways. There's no standing still on this journey of life.

In John 15:5, Jesus says, "I am the vine; you are the branches. If a man remains in me and I in him, he will bear much fruit; apart from me you can do nothing." Remaining in Jesus isn't a one-time thing. It has to become a lifestyle. We have to do it continually, or we become detached from the vine. In verse 6, Jesus continues, "If anyone does not remain in me, he is like a branch that is thrown away and withers; such branches are picked up, thrown into the fire and burned." If we don't remain in Him, the true vine, we will wither and die spiritually, and we won't be able to carry out His plans for our lives or find fulfillment in doing so.

What I'm talking about here isn't just another "self-help" thing. There's more to it than modifying your thoughts and behavior (although that is certainly a part of the whole.) It's not a "follow these steps and then you're free" sort-of thing. This is a God thing. We just have to surrender to His lordship and get our "selves" out of the way so He can work within us.

In Chapter ten we talked about being able to be content in all circumstances, good or bad. We looked at Philippians 4:11-12, which says, "I am not saying this because I am in need, for I have learned to be content whatever the circumstances. I know what it is to be in need, and I know what it is to have plenty. I have learned the secret of being content in any and every situation, whether well fed or hungry, whether living in plenty or in want."

There is another way to define "content" that I did not mention, but I want to now because it is very pertinent to our topic. The word for "content" here is a compound word that is literally translated "to ward off self."[1] "Ward" means, "to avert, repel, or turn aside (danger, harm, an attack, an assailant, etc.)"[2] Ward is very much an action word that takes effort. It's a battling word. We literally have to fight off our "self", our will, our pride, our desire for control, in order to find true freedom. True joy.

Freedom ain't free. It will cost you everything. Everything you think you are, everything you think you want for yourself or your loved ones. It will cost you control of your life. Coming to the place where you can accept this and start the battle of warding off your "self" and surrendering it to Jesus is where true freedom starts. Freedom from the *angst* that comes from trying to fight for control of your own life, from fighting to control the lives of your loved ones, however well-intentioned that control may be. Freedom from the grief and pain of the shattered dreams of the past.

When you give up the fight for control, let it go, and trust that God really does love you and has your best interests at heart, you reach the place of *acceptance*. The place of freedom. When you live your life in this state of freedom, following God's plan not yours, your dreams have the potential to come to fruition. Now you know the secret. It's time for you to find your new dream and go out be who God made you to be!

DISCUSSION QUESTIONS

1. Have you allowed God to begin the sanctification process in your heart and life?

2. Are there any difficult areas that you still need to surrender to the lordship of Christ?

3. What is your biggest takeaway from reading this book?

END NOTES

INTRODUCTION

1. "Random House Unabridged Dictionary 2020." Dictionary. com. Random House Inc. Accessed October 23, 2020. https:// www.dictionary.com/browse/miscarriage?s=t

2. "Random House Unabridged Dictionary 2020." Dictionary. com. Random House Inc. Accessed June 3, 2020. https://www. dictionary.com/browse/angst?s=t

3. Merriam-Webster.com Dictionary, S.V. "angst," accessed June 3, 2020. https://www.merriam-webster.com/dictionary/angst

CHAPTER ONE

1. Douglas A. Riley, *What Your Explosive Child is Trying to Tell You* (Boston-New York: Houghton Mifflin Company, 2008), 13.

2. Dr. Les Carter, *Imperative People* (Nashville: Thomas Nelson Publishers, 1991)

CHAPTER TWO

None

CHAPTER THREE

1. James Strong, LL.D., S.T.D., *The New Strong's Exhaustive Concordance of the Bible* (Nashville: Thomas Nelson Publishers, 1996) 98, Greek 5479.

CHAPTER FOUR

1. John L. Phillips, Jr., *Piaget's Theory: A Primer* (San Francisco: W. H. Freeman and Company, 1981), 67-96, 160.
2. Aaron Karmin, "Egocentric Guilt," May 22, 2018, http://www.blogs.psychcentral.com/anger/2018/05/egocentricguilt/
3. Dr. Caroline Leaf, *Who Switched Off My Brain?* (Southlake: Inprov, Ltd, 2009)

CHAPTER FIVE

None

CHAPTER SIX

1. Brian Wu, "Situational Depression or Clinical Depression?" *Medical News Today*, September 28, 2018, http://www.medicalnewstoday.com/articles/314698.php
2. Brene Brown, *The Gifts of Imperfection* (Center City: Hazelden, 2010)

CHAPTER SEVEN

1. Brian Wu, "Situational Depression or Clinical Depression?" *Medical News Today*, September 28, 2018, http://www.medicalnewstoday.com/articles/314698.php

CHAPTER EIGHT

None

CHAPTER NINE

1. James Strong, LL.D., S.T.D., *The New Strong's Exhaustive Concordance of the Bible* (Nashville: Thomas Nelson Publishers, 1996), 34, Greek 1950.
2. June Hunt, *Seeing Yourself Through God's Eyes* (Eugene: Harvest House Publishers, 2008)

3. Joyce Meyer, *Battlefield of the Mind* (Tulsa: Harrison House, Inc., 1995)

CHAPTER TEN

1. "Random House Unabridged Dictionary 2020." Dictionary. com. Random House Inc. Accessed June 3, 2020. http://www. dictionary.com/browse/content?s=t

2. Horatio Spafford, *It Is Well With My Soul*, 1873.

3. "Random House Unabridged Dictionary 2020." Dictionary. com. Random House Inc. Accessed June 3, 2020. http://www. dictionary.com/browse/trust?s=t

4. James Strong, LL.D., S.T.D., *The New Strong's Exhaustive Concordance of the Bible* (Nashville: Thomas Nelson Publishers, 1996), 18 Hebrew 982.

5. "Random House Unabridged Dictionary 2020." Dictionary. com. Random House Inc. Accessed June 3, 2020. http://www. dictionary.com/browse/yield?s=t

6. James Strong, LL.D., S.T.D., *The New Strong's Exhaustive Concordance of the Bible* (Nashville: Thomas Nelson Publishers, 1996), 94 Greek 5293.

7. James Strong, LL.D., S.T.D., *The New Strong's Exhaustive Concordance of the Bible* (Nashville: Thomas Nelson Publishers, 1996), 39 Greek 2218.

8. "Random House Unabridged Dictionary 2020." Dictionary. com. Random House Inc. Accessed June 3, 2020. http://www. dictionary.com/browse/yoke?s=t

CHAPTER ELEVEN

1. "Co-Dependency." Mental Health America. Accessed June 3,2020 http://www.mhanational.org/issues/co-dependency

CHAPTER TWELVE

1. Spiros Zodhiates, Th.D., *The Complete Word Study Dictionary New Testament* (Chattanooga: AMG Publishers, 1992), 408.

2. "Random House Unabridged Dictionary 2020." Dictionary. com. Random House Inc. Accessed June 3, 2020. http://www. dictionary.com/browse/despot?s=t

CHAPTER THIRTEEN

None

CHAPTER FOURTEEN

1. "Random House Unabridged Dictionary 2020." Dictionary. com. Random House Inc. Accessed June 3, 2020. http://www. dictionary.com/browse/freedom?s=t

CHAPTER FIFTEEN

1. James Strong, LL.D., S.T.D., *The New Strong's Exhaustive Concordance of the Bible* (Nashville: Thomas Nelson Publishers, 1996), 15 Greek 842.
2. "Random House Unabridged Dictionary 2020." Dictionary. com. Random House Inc. Accessed June 3, 2020. http://www. dictionary.com/browse/ward=t

Want to continue your healing journey but you're not sure how?

I would love to help you further.
Contact me at:
www.kristilarrabee.com
or
www.facebook.com/
Kristi-Larrabee-Author-367743013302314

to learn more about my other services.